BISEXUALITY
Making the Invisible Visible
in Faith Communities

Marie Alford-Harkey and Rev. Debra W. Haffner

RELIGIOUS INSTITUTE

Religious Institute
21 Charles Street
Suite 140
Westport, CT 06880

Printed in the United States of America

ISBN 978-0-9855949-3-0

For more information, visit www.religiousinstitute.org.

ACKNOWLEDGEMENTS

Many people and organizations made important contributions to the development of this guidebook.

The guide began with a colloquium on bisexuality held in April, 2013. The participants who generously contributed their time and expertise were Imam Daaiyee Abdullah, Muslims for Progressive Values; Rev. Dr. Kelly Brown Douglas, Goucher College; Rev. Dr. Janet Edwards, Presbyterian Minister, PCUSA; Rev. Cedric A. Harmon, Many Voices; Zr. Alex Kapitan, Unitarian Universalist Association of Congregations; Rabbi Debra Kolodny, Nehirim and P'Nai Or of Portland, OR; Ms. Lacey Louwagie, co-editor of *Hungering and Thirsting for Justice: True Stories by Young Adult Catholics*; Ms. Denise Penn, American Institute of Bisexuality; Dr. Ritch C. Savin-Williams, Cornell University; Rev. Michael Schuenemeyer, United Church of Christ; Rev. Dr. John Selders, Interdenominational Conference of Liberation Congregations and Ministries, International; Rabbi Dr. Mychal Springer, Jewish Theological Seminary; and Mr. John Sylla, American Institute of Bisexuality.

The Religious Institute is grateful to the scientists and theologians who reviewed initial drafts of this guidebook. They are Rev. Dr. Janet Edwards, Rev. Cedric A. Harmon, Zr. Alex Kapitan, Rabbi Debra Kolodny, Ms. Lacey Louwagie, Dr. Ritch Savin-Williams, Rev. Michael Schuenemeyer, Rev. Darryl Stephens, and John Sylla; as well as to Marisa Procopio for editing, and design by Alan Barnett Design.

As noted in the section on religious traditions, writers from different traditions contributed thoughtful pieces on bisexuality. We are grateful to Imam Daaiyee Abdullah; Rev. Dr. Kelly Brown Douglas; Chaplain Allison Kestenbaum, Jewish Theological Seminary; Rabbi Debra Kolodny; Rev. Will McGarvey, Community Presbyterian Church of Pittsburg, CA; and Dr. Kate M. Ott, Drew Theological School, for their essays.

Many people contributed stories for our case studies. They include Rev. Dr. Janet Edwards, Ms. Lacey Louwagie, Rev. Summer Shaud, and several clergy and lay people who gave permission to publish their stories anonymously.

We are especially thankful to our friends and colleagues who identify as bisexual and who were infinitely patient as we discussed this work with them and sought their input. The book is much richer for their contributions, questions, and challenges.

The funding for the development and publication of *Bisexuality: Making the Invisible Visible in Faith Communities* was provided by the American Institute of Bisexuality. We are grateful for their support of this project and for their encouragement of the Religious Institute's mission to advocate for sexual health, education, and justice in faith communities and society.

RELIGIOUS DECLARATION ON SEXUAL MORALITY, JUSTICE, AND HEALING

Sexuality is God's life-giving and life-fulfilling gift. We come from diverse religious communities to recognize sexuality as central to our humanity and as integral to our spirituality. We are speaking out against the pain, brokenness, oppression and loss of meaning that many experience about their sexuality.

Our faith traditions celebrate the goodness of creation, including our bodies and our sexuality. We sin when this sacred gift is abused or exploited. However, the great promise of our traditions is love, healing and restored relationships.

Our culture needs a sexual ethic focused on personal relationships and social justice rather than particular sexual acts. All persons have the right and responsibility to lead sexual lives that express love, justice, mutuality, commitment, consent and pleasure. Grounded in respect for the body and for the vulnerability that intimacy brings, this ethic fosters physical, emotional and spiritual health. It accepts no double standards and applies to all persons, without regard to sex, gender, color, age, bodily condition, marital status or sexual orientation.

God hears the cries of those who suffer from the failure of religious communities to address sexuality. We are called today to see, hear and respond to the suffering caused by sexual abuse and violence against women and lesbian, gay, bisexual and transgender (LGBT) persons, the HIV pandemic, unsustainable population growth and over-consumption, and the commercial exploitation of sexuality.

Faith communities must therefore be truth-seeking, courageous and just. We call for:
- Theological reflection that integrates the wisdom of excluded, often silenced peoples, and insights about sexuality from medicine, social science, the arts and humanities.
- Full inclusion of women and LGBT persons in congregational life, including their ordination and marriage equality.
- Sexuality counseling and education throughout the lifespan from trained religious leaders.
- Support for those who challenge sexual oppression and who work for justice within their congregations and denominations.

Faith communities must also advocate for sexual and spiritual wholeness in society. We call for:
- Lifelong, age-appropriate sexuality education in schools, seminaries, and community settings.
- A faith-based commitment to sexual and reproductive rights, including access to voluntary contraception, abortion, and HIV/STI prevention and treatment.
- Religious leadership in movements to end sexual and social injustice.

God rejoices when we celebrate our sexuality with holiness and integrity.

TABLE OF CONTENTS

INTRODUCTION

*I*magine the following situations in your faith community:

- A congregant comes to you for pastoral counseling. He is excited, yet distressed that although he has always identified as straight, he has fallen in love with someone of the same sex.
- You are on the search committee for a new pastor in your community. One of the applicant's profiles states that she identifies as bisexual.
- A married woman in your congregation finds explicit homoerotic websites on her husband's computer and comes to you for advice.
- A person everyone believes to be gay comes to a congregation party holding hands with a person of another sex.
- Two middle school students in the youth group announce that they are bisexual.

Is your faith community prepared for these situations? Is your faith community open to people whose sexuality does not fit into the categories of gay/lesbian or straight? Does your faith community have access to resources about bisexuality and bisexual people?

This guidebook is designed to help congregations understand bisexuality and to encourage faith communities to "make the invisible visible." Our hope is that religious leaders and congregations will use this guidebook to inspire theological reflection and action in their faith communities. Religious traditions vary in how they address sexuality issues. This guidebook is written to address the broad spectrum of American congregations. It is our hope that the information it contains will be relevant or adaptable to Jewish, Christian, Unitarian Universalist, and Islamic faith communities.

Part One of the book, "Bisexuality Basics," begins by naming the harm that many bisexual people suffer, and includes definitions of terms, models to help understand sexual orientation, research on bisexuality, information on the prevalence of bisexuality in the United States, and myths and facts about bisexuality.

Part Two, "Sacred Texts and Religious Traditions," introduces theological issues related to bisexuality, and includes a discussion of sexuality in the Hebrew and Christian Scriptures, essays authored by theologians from different traditions, and the few denominational policies that exist on bisexuality.

Part Three, "Creating a Bisexually Healthy Congregation," presents information and strategies for faith communities and religious leaders to become more welcoming and affirming of bisexual persons and others who are attracted to people of more than one sex or gender. Sections include welcoming and affirming bisexual persons, bisexually healthy religious professionals, worship resources, pastoral counseling, youth, social action, and a call to action.

Bisexuality is often invisible in lesbian, gay, bisexual, and transgender (LGBT) organizations, society as a whole, and in faith communities and denominations. Although many mainline denominations and congregations have made great strides in welcoming and affirming lesbian and gay people, and some have even begun to respond to the specific needs and concerns of transgender people, the "B" in the LGBT acronym is still largely ignored.

This guide defines bisexuality as "an enduring romantic, emotional and/or sexual attraction toward people of more than one sex or gender." It is quite likely that in all faith communities, there are people with bisexual attractions, feelings, behaviors, or identities. **People who fit into some category of bisexuality broadly defined (identity, attraction and/or behavior) make up the largest portion of the LGBT community in the United States.**[1]

For congregations, what is most important to recognize is that there are far more people who are attracted to and engage in behaviors with people of more than one sex or gender than is readily apparent. The welcome and inclusion of bisexual people will directly affect many more people than those who identify as bisexual. In addition, as stated in a British report on bisexual inclusion, "estimates of the bisexual population have no relation to the necessity of ensuring that bisexual people enjoy equality and freedom from discrimination: these rights apply to all regardless of sexual identity or attraction."[2]

Bisexual persons have suffered because of the failure of faith communities, LGBT communities, and society at large to fully embrace bisexuality as a distinct sexual orientation. Compared to people who are gay, lesbian, or straight, people who are bisexual are at greater risk for mental health issues, have greater sexual health risks, and face more stressors in daily life. In addition, bisexual youth are more likely than straight or gay/lesbian youth to engage in risky behaviors such as violence against others, attempted suicide, tobacco use, alcohol use, and other drug use. (See "Healing the Suffering" on p. 22 for more information.)

> The noble lover of beauty engages in love wherever he sees excellence and splendid natural endowment without regard for any difference in physiological detail…. The love of human beauty [will] be fairly and equally disposed toward both sexes, instead of supposing that males and females are as different in the matter of love as they are in their clothes.[3]
>
> — *Plutarch, Greek philosopher, 1st century, A.D.*

Helping faith communities embrace bisexual persons and reflect theologically on bisexuality brings gifts to congregations and to the practice of faith. When a congregation welcomes and recognizes people of all sexual orientations and gender identities, it contributes to a positive image of religion among people who may have rejected religion as intolerant or irrelevant. Such congregations become safe spaces for youth who are exploring their sexuality and have questions. In addition, embracing bisexual persons makes it possible for those persons to be open about their identity and helps create a more open atmosphere in the faith community, encouraging authenticity and community among members. Congregations that embrace bisexual persons can also help heal the suffering caused by the invisibility of bisexual people in society.

Our religious traditions call us to love our neighbor, to welcome the stranger, and to advocate on behalf of those whose voices often go unheard. It is our hope that this guidebook will foster those values in our communities through study and conversation.

Notes

1 Pew Research Center, Pew Research Social & Demographic Trends, "A Survey of LGBT Americans: Attitudes, Experiences, and Values in Changing Times," http://www.pewsocialtrends.org/2013/06/13/a-survey-of-lgbt-americans.

2 Meg Barker et al, "The Bisexuality Report: Bisexual Inclusion in LGBT Equality and Diversity," The Open University Centre for Citizenship, Identities and Governance and Faculty of Health and Social Care, http://www.open.ac.uk/ccig/files/ccig/The%20BisexualityReport%20Feb.2012.pdf.

3 Plutarch, *Dialogue on Love [Amatorius]*, trans. W.C. Helmhold (Cambridge, MA, 1961), p. 415.

PART ONE

BISEXUALITY BASICS

*Congregations and religious leaders need accurate
information in order to help create bisexually
healthy faith communities, yet few people
have had opportunities to inform themselves
about bisexuality. Facts, research, models, and
definitions can help people of faith who are
interested in sexual justice educate themselves.*

DEFINITIONS AND MODELS
OF SEXUAL ORIENTATION

*T*oday, researchers understand that sexual orientation is more complex than sexual behaviors alone. The Religious Institute defines sexual orientation as an individual's enduring romantic, emotional, or sexual attractions toward other persons. Sexual orientation is a complex relationship among sexual attractions, behaviors, and self-identity.[1]

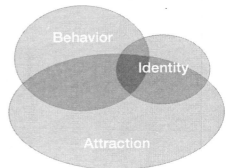

"Heterosexual," "homosexual," and "bisexual" are examples of specific sexual orientations. Sexual orientation refers to feelings and identity, not just behavior. Individuals do not always express their sexual orientation through their sexual behaviors.

The purpose of this guide is to help congregations welcome a range of people who are attracted in varying degrees to people of more than one sex or gender. This guide defines bisexuality as "an enduring romantic, emotional and/or sexual attraction toward people of more than one sex or gender."

A bisexual person may be attracted to one sex or gender more than another, equally attracted to all sexes and genders, or may consider sex and gender unimportant in terms of their sexual and romantic attractions. The intensity of a bisexual person's attractions toward one sex or gender or another may vary over time.[2]

Some bisexuals have not had sexual behaviors with another person. Others have had only same-sex experiences or have been only with partners of a different sex or gender from their own. As described in the "Prevalence of Bisexuality in the United States" section on p. 18, many people who identify as lesbian, heterosexual, gay, or another label have had sex with partners of more than one sex or gender.

Some people have been identified in the professional literature as "mostly heterosexual." These are people who identify as heterosexual but who also have "a small degree of same-sex sexuality in at least one…indicator of sexual orientation (sexual/romantic attraction, arousal, fantasy, infatuation, and identity)."[3]

For some people, gender expression and gender identity are also factors in sexual attraction. For some bisexuals, gender is an important part of attraction. For other bisexuals, it is totally irrelevant. And to make things even more complex, some people are bisexual throughout their life while others find that their sexual and romantic attractions change during different periods of their lives.

Those who are attracted to people of more than one sex or gender may use a variety of words to describe their sexual orientation, including bisexual, "bi," same and other gender loving, pansexual, ambisexual, omnisexual, fluid, and queer. There is no one word that everyone agrees captures the complexity of the range of sexual orientations. **For the purposes of this guide, the words *bisexual* and *bisexuality* will be used.**

This guide will address how congregations can better serve people who identify as bisexual as well as people who experience a range of sexual attractions, feelings, or behaviors with people of more than one sex or gender without identifying as bisexual.

MODELS TO HELP UNDERSTAND THE RANGE OF SEXUAL ORIENTATIONS

In order to have a greater understanding about bisexuality, it is important to understand the complexity of sexual orientation. Many models of sexual orientation have been developed by researchers, social scientists and advocates over the past fifty years.

The Kinsey Scale

In 1948, the sexuality research-er Alfred Kinsey and his col-leagues proposed a seven-point scale for sexual orientation based on an individual's overt sexual experience and/or psy-chosexual reactions, although Kinsey's research focused on behaviors.[4] The Kinsey Insti-tute now describes the scale this way: "The scale ranges

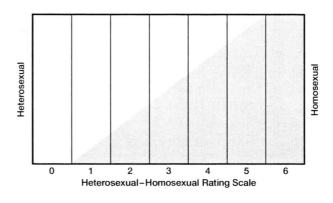

from 0, for those who would identify themselves as exclusively heterosexual with no experience with or desire for sexual activity with their same sex, to 6, for those who would identify themselves as exclusively homosexual with no experience with or desire for sexual activity with those of the opposite sex, and 1–5 for those who would identify themselves with varying levels of desire or sexual activity with either sex."[5] Kinsey's 1948 report on American men estimated that 46% were in the range of 1–5 at some point in their lives.[6]

Kinsey described each point on the scale as follows:

0 – Exclusively heterosexual with no homosexual
1 – Predominantly heterosexual, only incidentally homosexual
2 – Predominantly heterosexual, but more than incidentally homosexual
3 – Equally heterosexual and homosexual
4 – Predominantly homosexual, but more than incidentally heterosexual
5 – Predominantly homosexual, only incidentally heterosexual
6 – Exclusively homosexual

Limitations of the Kinsey Scale

While the Kinsey scale was revolutionary at its publication in advancing the understanding of sexual orientation as a spectrum, it has significant limitations, especially in its conception of bisexuality. The Kinsey scale could imply (and has been used to assert) that the only "true bisexuals" are those who have sexual behaviors equally with men and women. Instead of expressly using the term "bisexual," the Kinsey scale uses the terms "heterosexual" and "homosexual," even for people with behaviors in the 1 to 5 range. The Kinsey scale is also a linear scale that does not account for the possibility of changes over time, or the interaction of one's own gender expression and identity with sexual attraction. It conflates the many dimensions of sexual orientation into a single number, whereas people may differ in the erotic, romantic, and affectional components of their sexual orientation.

The Klein Sexual Orientation Grid

Several decades later, building on the work of Dr. Kinsey and his colleagues, Dr. Fritz Klein developed a more nuanced two-dimensional model of sexual orientation, now known as the Klein Sexual Orientation Grid. It was first published in his book, *The Bisexual Option*, in 1978. The Klein Grid is designed to expand on Kinsey's work in several ways. First, it accounts for the fact that a person's sexual orientation may change over time, and asks people to rate their past, present, and ideal orientation on each factor. The Klein Grid includes seven variables that use a 1 to 7 rating criteria similar to the Kinsey scale, ranging from exclusive "opposite" sex attraction to exclusive same sex attraction. The 21 boxes are rated, and then can be viewed as a complex individual picture that cannot be reduced to a single number on a one-dimensional scale. The variables are:

- Sexual Attraction — to whom an individual is sexually attracted
- Sexual Behavior — with whom an individual engages in sexual behaviors
- Sexual Fantasies — about whom one has fantasies
- Emotional Preference — with whom one falls in love
- Social Preference — the sex of the people with whom one socializes

- Lifestyle Preference — sexual identity of the people with whom one socializes
- Sexual Identity — how an individual self-identifies[7]

Klein Sexual Orentation Grid

	Past	Present	Ideal Future
Sexual Attraction			
SexualBehavior			
Sexual Fantasies			
Emotional Preference			
Social Preference			
Heterosexual-Homosexual Lifestyle			
Self-Identification			

Although some of the terms that Klein uses (such as "lifestyle" or "preference") are outdated today, his insights that sexual orientation is composed of many variables that may fall at different places in Kinsey's continuum and that sexual orientation is "an ongoing dynamic process" help explain the complexity of sexual orientation in a way that Kinsey's model did not.

AER (Affectional/Erotic/Romantic) Model

Wayne Pawlowski, an AASECT-certified sexuality educator, created the AER model to address the complex interplay between affectional feelings, erotic feelings, and romantic feelings. He labeled these as affectional orientation, erotic orientation, and romantic orientation. The model is based on the following open-ended questions:

A: Affectional orientation: "With whom do you prefer to socialize? With which sex(es) do you feel most comfortable and relaxed?"

E: Erotic orientation: "Which sex(es) turn(s) you on erotically? To whom are you attracted as real, potential, or fantasy sexual partners?"

R: Romantic orientation: "With whom do you fall in love? With whom do you fall in love most easily?"

It is common to assume that these three areas are the same or at least closely related, but Pawlowski cautions that they can be three separate and distinct aspects of sexual orientation.

In fact, he suggests that what we call "sexual orientation" is actually a complex interplay of an individual's affectional, erotic and romantic orientations working in concert with one another, not simply to whom one is attracted erotically.

Consider, for example, a man married to a woman—and the man periodically has sexual encounters with other men. Although some might assume he is gay, he indeed could be romantically in love with his wife and socially much more comfortable being in a relationship with a woman. His erotic attractions could fall anywhere from a Kinsey 1 to a 6, but his affectional and romantic attractions could indicate a bisexual orientation.

The AER model is completely different from the Kinsey Scale and the Klein Grid in that it doesn't depend on a two-dimensional continuum of orientation. Instead, it asks open-ended questions. It allows for the possibility that a person may actually answer "no one" to the questions pertaining to one or more of the three orientations. Further, it allows for gender diversity in a way that previous models did not.

Pawlowski suggests that of the three orientations, affectional is the most influenced by environment/upbringing/life experience. The other two orientations (erotic and romantic) tend to be far less influenced by environment.[8]

In my congregation, I discovered that writing about my coming out…was really just the beginning. Not a single person in my church has reacted negatively to my coming out (at least not that I'm aware of), but for many, it prompted curiosity and a desire to know more and better understand. So in the weeks that followed, I had a number of conversation with parishioners and fellow staff members who wanted me to provide a kind of "bisexuality 101." Those conversations were sometimes awkward for me, but they were clearly and invariably coming from a place of love and a sincere desire to understand.

— *Rev. Summer Shaud, Associate Pastor, First Congregational Church, Natick, MA*

Definitions

Asexual: Experiencing little or no romantic, emotional and/or sexual attraction or eroticism. Asexuality is different from celibacy, which is a choice not to engage in sexual behaviors with another person.

Biological sex: Biological status as female, male, or intersex. It is determined by a person's sexual anatomy, chromosomes, and hormones. Biological sex is often referred to as "sex" or "natal sex."[9]

Biphobia: Fear or hatred of bisexuals, sometimes manifesting in discrimination, isolation, harassment, or violence. Often biphobia is based on inaccurate stereotypes, including associations with infidelity, promiscuity, and transmission of sexually transmitted diseases.[10]

Bisexual: Experiencing enduring romantic, emotional and/or sexual attraction toward people of more than one sex or gender.

Gender: The collection of characteristics that form the cultural constructs that define people as boys/men, girls/women, or other.

Gender expression: The outward expression (behavior, clothing, hairstyle, voice or body characteristics) of a particular gender role and/or identity.

Gender identity: An individual's internal sense of self as boy/man, girl/woman, or other. Gender identity may or may not align with an individual's biological sex, and may or may not be accurately perceived externally.

Gender roles: A set of social and behavioral norms that determine what is generally considered appropriate for either a man or a woman in a social or interpersonal relationship.

LGBT: An acronym for "lesbian, gay, bisexual and transgender." Lengthier versions include "LGBTQ" to include people who identify as "queer," and "LGBTQQIA," to include "queer, questioning, intersex and asexual." The "A" may also be used to refer to "allies" or "advocates," i.e., people who support justice for LGBT persons.

BI-FRIENDLY

Throughout this guidebook, we use the term "bi-friendly" to refer to organizations, events, websites, print materials, and healthcare and other service providers who are knowledgeable about and welcoming to persons who identify as bisexual, who have bisexual attractions, and/or who engage in bisexual behaviors.

Questioning: A term used to describe people who are unsure of or exploring their sexual orientation and/or gender identity.

Sexuality: The sexual knowledge, beliefs, attitudes, values and behaviors of individuals. Its dimensions include the anatomy, physiology and biochemistry of the sexual response and reproductive systems; gender identity, sexual orientation, roles and personality; as well as thoughts, attachments, physical and emotional expressions, and relationships.

Sexual identity: An individual's sense of self as a sexual being, including natal sex, gender identity, gender role, gender expression, sexual orientation and sexual self-concept. Sexual identify may also refer to the language and labels people use to define themselves. Sexual self-concept refers to one's assessment of one's sexual identity.

Transgender: A term for individuals whose gender identity or expression differs from the cultural expectations of their biological sex. Some people transition from male to female or from female to male, often taking steps to align their biological sex and their gender expression with their gender identity. Other people do not identify as women or men; they might identify as a little of both or as a different gender entirely. The term "transgender" does not provide information about a person's sexual orientation; transgender people may identify as gay, lesbian, heterosexual, bisexual, or another sexual orientation.

❧

WHAT'S THE RIGHT WORD?

Choosing words carefully can help counter bisexual invisibility and prejudice. Here are some common examples to consider.

Use	Avoid
lesbian, gay, bisexual, transgender	"gay/lesbian" to represent all LGBT people
bisexual	bi-sexual, switch-hitter
anti-LGBT bias	anti-gay bias
different sex couple, other sex couple	opposite sex couple
marriage equality	"gay" marriage
questioning	bi-curious
LGBT rights, human rights	gay rights

If you want to know how people identify, ask, and then use the terms they prefer. Avoid making assumptions about sexual orientation based on the sex or gender of a person's partners. Peoples' definitions of terms describing sexual orientation and gender identity may vary, and all individuals have the right to define themselves and to have that definition respected by others.

Questions for Reflection

1. Do the models of sexual orientation aid your understanding? What is most helpful? Is there anything that is still unclear to you? Where might you seek additional information?

2. How comfortable are you in using the terms in the definitions section? Do you need information about any other terms?

3. When did you first encounter the term *bisexual*? Was it in a positive context or a negative context? What messages (if any) did you receive as a child, adolescent, and young adult about bisexuality?

4. When you hear the words *bisexual* and *bisexuality*, what images come to mind? How might you learn more?

5. What difference does it make when your congregation says "LGBT" rather than "lesbian, gay, bisexual and transgender"? Do people hear the "B" in LGBT?

6. How can the language used in your congregation and faith community be more inclusive of people who have bisexual experience or identity?

Notes

1 Illustration of components of sexual orientation by John Sylla, President of the American Institute of Bisexuality.

2 Timothy and Palmer and Rev. Debra W. Haffner, *A Time to Seek: Study Guide on Sexual and Gender Diversity* (Westport, CT: Religious Institute, 2007).

3 Ritch C. Savin-Williams and Zhana Vrangalova, "Mostly Heterosexual as a Distinct Sexual Orientation Group: A Systematic Review of the Empirical Evidence," *Developmental Review* 33 (2013): 58–88.

4 Robert T. Francoeur, *The Complete Dictionary of Sexology*, ed. (New York: Continuum, 1995), 329.

5 The Kinsey Institute, "Kinsey's Heterosexual-Homosexual Rating Scale," http://www.kinseyinstitute.org/research/ak-hhscale.html.

6 Alfred C. Kinsey, *Sexual Behavior in the Human Male* (Bloomington, IN: Indiana University Press, 1998). Originally published by W.B. Saunders Company, 1948.

7 Fritz Klein, M.D., "The Klein Sexual Orientation Grid," American Institute of Bisexuality, http://www.americaninstituteofbisexuality.org/thekleingrid/.

8 Wayne Pawlowski, in discussion with the authors, May 29, 2013.

9 Planned Parenthood, *Female, Male, & Intersex*, http://www.plannedparenthood.org/health-topics/sexual-orientation-gender/female-male-intersex-26531.htm.

10 San Francisco Human Rights Commission, *Bisexual Invisibility*, http://sf-hrc.org/index.aspx?page=128#LGBT and Intersex Communities, 2011, p. 35.

MYTHS AND FACTS ABOUT BISEXUALITY

Many people, including people of faith and religious leaders, have incomplete information about bisexuality. There are many myths in the media and in popular culture about bisexuality. These myths are often based on inaccurate and harmful stereotypes, including associating bisexuals with infidelity, promiscuity, and transmission of sexually transmitted diseases.[1]

MYTH: *Bisexuality is a phase that people go through before identifying as gay or lesbian.*

FACT: Research has demonstrated that bisexuality is an enduring and distinct sexual orientation. Although some people do identify themselves as bisexual in their teens and early adult years as a way to become more comfortable with their same-sex attractions, many people understand their orientation as bisexual throughout their lives.[2, 3]

MYTH: *Bisexuality doesn't exist. People who say they are bisexual are either afraid to come out as gay or lesbian, or they are actually straight and just want to appear "hip."*

FACT: Research has shown that bisexuality is a distinct sexual orientation, and that many people experience romantic and sexual desires and attractions toward people of different sexes and genders.

MYTH: *Only young people/white people/women/insert-identifier-here are bisexual.*

FACT: Bisexual people exist in all cultures, age groups, racial and ethnic groups, and gender identities.

MYTH: *If a bisexual person marries a person of another sex, they are no longer bisexual.*

FACT: One's sexual orientation doesn't change just because one is in a relationship. There are people in long-term, committed, monogamous relationships with someone of another sex who continue to identify as bisexual. The converse is true for bisexual people in same-sex relationships.

MYTH: *Bisexual people spread HIV by having sex with both men and women; bisexual women spread AIDS to the lesbian community and bisexual men spread HIV to the heterosexual community.*

FACT: HIV infection and AIDS occur in people of all sexual orientations. Unprotected sexual behaviors increase the risk of the spread of HIV, not a person's sexual orientation.

MYTH: *Bisexual people in relationships with other-sex partners are taking advantage of "straight privilege."*

FACT: It is true that in a culture that privileges heterosexuality and/or assumes that everyone is heterosexual (which is known as heteronormativity), it is easier to have a partner of another sex. However, bisexual people fall in love with a partner based on character, attractions, chemistry, and shared values — just like straight, lesbian, and gay people do — rather than based on which life will be easier. Partnered bisexual people often experience similar issues related to being "closeted" as lesbians and gay men and may experience the additional issue of feeling invisible based on the sex or gender of their partner.

MYTH: *If a person has not had sexual experiences with people of more than one sex or gender, that person is not "really" bisexual.*

FACT: As described on pp. 6–10, sexual orientation consists of many different dimensions, including sexual attraction, behaviors and fantasies, romantic feelings, erotic attraction, and self-identity. One has a right to label one's own identity. People can know they are bisexual without having had sex with anyone at all.

MYTH: *Bisexual people are promiscuous and incapable of being monogamous.*

FACT: Bisexual people are just as likely to be faithful to their commitments as non-bisexual people. According to Dr. Lisa Diamond, "In reality, a great many bisexual individuals have happily monogamous relationships with their partners." For example, at the end of a ten-year study, 89% of women who identified as bisexual were in monogamous, long-term relationships.[5]

MYTH: *Gay and lesbian people are totally accepting of bisexuality. It's only straight people who have a problem with it.*

FACT: Bisexual people can be discriminated against by heterosexual, lesbian, and gay people. Some gay and lesbian organizations ignore the needs or even the existence of bisexuals or reinforce the myth that all bisexuals are really gay or lesbian.

The "privilege" of passing possessed by invisible minorities also carries as its counterweight the onus of having to actively announce one's identity group membership in order to avoid being assumed to be other than one is, as well as feelings of guilt or discomfort that may arise when one is silent. If we are silent or neutral, we are subject to misinterpretation, invisibility, and even the perception that we do not exist at all. We carry the weight of constantly having to make the decision of how and when to come out, and at what cost.[4]

— *Robyn Ochs, Bisexual Advocate*

And a final myth...

MYTH: *Congregations that say they are welcoming of LGBT people are fully welcoming, inclusive, and affirming of bisexual people.*

FACT: Although many denominations and their congregations have adopted the acronym "LGBT" in their welcoming statements, it is very common for the policies and practices of such denominations and congregations to be more inclusive of lesbian and gay people than bisexual people or transgender people. Clergy and congregations need to be aware that there are unique issues affecting bisexual people that are different from those affecting people who are gay or lesbian. Congregations also need to identify their commitments to lesbian, gay, bisexual, and transgender people explicitly instead of always using the acronym "LGBT." For more ideas on fully including and welcoming bisexual people, see the section on "Welcoming and Affirming Bisexual People in Congregations," pp. 54–57.

One pastor friend invited me to have coffee after he heard from someone else that I am bi. He wanted to warn me that adultery is prohibited by one of the Ten Commandments. He cared enough about me to speak to me. He assumed that I had to be promiscuous because I identify as bisexual. When I figured out what he was talking about, I assured him that I am faithful to my husband. I realized that when he had learned I'm bi, I had become a stranger to him, and it took this conversation to keep our friendship going. Suddenly, I had to explain myself and, sadly, reassure a friend that my being bi did not mean I was any different from how I had always been: faithful, committed, myself.

— Rev. Dr. Janet Edwards, Presbyterian minister

Questions for Reflection

1. Have you heard any of these myths? Do the facts change your mind?

2. How do these myths hurt bisexual people? How can your congregation counter such myths?

3. If you hear someone repeat one of these myths, what could you do or say? Are you comfortable being an ally and an outspoken bystander to counter biphobia?

Notes

1 San Francisco Human Rights Commission, *Bisexual Invisibility,* http://sf-hrc.org/index
.aspx?page=128#LGBT and Intersex Communities, (2011), p. 35.

2 Lisa M. Diamond, "Female Bisexuality from Adolescence to Adulthood: Results From a 10-year
Longitudinal Study," *Developmental Psychology* 44 (2008): pp. 5–14.

3 Jerome A. Cerny and Erik Janssen, "Patterns of Sexual Arousal in Homosexual, Bisexual, and
Heterosexual Men," *Archives of Sexual Behavior* 40 (2011):687–697.

4 Robyn Ochs, "Biphobia: It Goes More Than Two Ways," http://www.robynochs.com/writing/essays/
biphobia.html.

5 Lisa M. Diamond, *Female Bisexuality,* 5–14.

PREVALENCE OF BISEXUALITY IN THE UNITED STATES

For many reasons, it is hard to estimate the number of bisexual people in the United States. This is in part because bisexuality is complex and difficult to define. In addition, many people who engage in sexual behaviors with people of different sexes or genders do not identify as bisexual. In contrast, some people who are romantically and/or sexually attracted to people of more than one sex do not engage in bisexual behaviors and/or do not identify as bisexual.

There have been a number of recent national studies that have asked adults and adolescents about how they identify their sexual orientation, their sexual attractions, and the sex of their sexual partners in the past year and over their lifetime. Although more than nine in ten Americans identify as heterosexual, significant numbers of Americans identify as another sexual orientation. (See table.) Depending on which variable is used, the percentage of people in the United States who could be considered bisexual ranges from 1.2% to 16% of the general population — as many as 50 million people in the United States.

The percentage of people who fit into some category of bisexuality broadly defined (identity, attraction and/or behavior) makes up the largest portion of the LGBT community. A 2013 survey of lesbian, gay, bisexual, and transgender adults in the United States by the Pew Research Center found that 40% of LGBT individuals surveyed identified as bisexual.[1] A 2011 survey solely of transgender people in the United States by the National Gay and Lesbian Task Force and the National Center for Transgender Equality found that 25% of transgender people identified as bisexual.[2]

Several studies found that women are much more likely than men to identify as bisexual, especially younger sexually active women. In the Pew Center survey of LGBT adults, 73% of those who identified as bisexual were women.[3]

In 2010, researchers at Indiana University (IU) conducted a national probability sample study of sexual behaviors in the United States. Almost 3% of men and 3.6% of women identified as bisexual. Teen boys were less likely to identify as gay or bisexual than adult men; teen women, conversely, were less likely to identify as lesbian but much more likely to identify as bisexual than adult women in the study.

Sexual Orientation by Self-Identification	Adults		Older Teens*	
	Men	Women	Men	Women
Bisexual	1%	4%	1%	6–8%
Lesbian/Gay	2–4%	1%	2%	1–2%
Heterosexual	92%–96%	93%–94%	96%–97%	90%

Sexual Attractions to Same Sex, Other Sex, More Than One Sex	Only opposite sex	Mostly opposite sex	Equally to both	Mostly same sex	Only same sex
Women	83%	12%	3%	.6%	.8%
Men	94%	4%	.5%	.7%	1%

Same-Sex Attractions and Behaviors	Men	Women
Any same-sex attractions	5%	15%
Any same-sex behaviors (lifetime)	5–15%	12–14%
Same-sex behaviors in the past year	4%	12%

*Teens are 18–19 years old in NSFG data, 14–19 in IU data.

All numbers in tables are rounded. See text for exact figures. Tables combine data from these two studies:
• Chandra, Mosher, and Copen, *Sexual Behavior.*
• Herbenick et al, *Sexual Behavior in the United States.*

The National Survey of Family Growth (2006–2010) (NSFG), conducted by the National Center for Health Statistics (part of the Centers for Disease Control and Prevention), also asked questions about sexual orientation, including questions about self-identity, sexual behaviors, and sexual attractions.

Among men and women ages 18–44, the NSFG found that 3.9% of women identify as bisexual, as do 1.2% of men.[4] However, the data for sexual attraction gives a fuller picture. The survey asked people to describe their sexual attraction to others as "only opposite sex," "mostly opposite sex," "equally to both," "mostly same sex," "only same sex," or "not sure." Women were five times more likely to identify as being attracted in at least some degree to people of both sexes. Sixteen percent of women report some attraction to "both sexes," although just under 5% of men do so.[5]

In both studies, younger women were more likely to identify as bisexual than older women and more likely to have engaged in sexual behaviors with a same-sex partner than older women or men of any age. Sixteen percent of women ages 20 to 24 report that they have shared intimate sexual experiences with another woman at some point and 15% had done so in the past year. Only 1% of women ages 35 to 44 identify as bisexual while 5.8% of teen women ages 18 to 19 and 6.3% of women ages 20 to 24 do so. Among men, no such differences exist by age.

Complicating prevalence estimates further, Ritch Savin-Williams and Zhana Vrangalova, researchers from Cornell University, have concluded that evidence supports a distinct sexual orientation called "mostly heterosexual." These individuals have "a small degree of same-sex sexual and/or romantic attraction and, occasionally, same-sex behavior." They have also concluded that this orientation remains relatively stable over time.[6] The NSFG study found that nearly one in eight women and one in twenty-five men would fit into this "mostly heterosexual" orientation as defined by sexual attraction.

Why is it important to know how many people are bisexual? A significant number of people in the United States fit into some category of bisexuality (identity, attraction, and/or behavior), and thus represent a significant number of people in most congregations. The percentages of older teens and young adults who identify as bisexual or who have engaged in sexual behaviors with more than one sex is higher than in the past and may reflect a growing openness about sexuality in the culture. For congregations, what is most important to recognize is that there are far more people who are attracted to and engage in behaviors with people of more than one sex or gender than is readily apparent. The welcome and inclusion of bisexual people will directly affect many more people than those who identify as bisexual.

I am a happily married, out bisexual man. I'm a parent, and I'm a Presbyterian pastor. It took me a long time to be honest with myself about being bisexual. It's easy to pass as a bi person. I had the normal crushes of childhood and adolescence but I also found myself attracted to a spectrum of people. I knew I wanted a family and it was natural for me to fall in love with Becky and start a family. In many ways, being a married man, it would have been easier just to stay in the closet.

I have found that the time I spent not being out as a bi man was a form of lying, of bearing false witness against myself and a loving God. For years this led to hiding my solidarity from those who needed to encounter it the most. Sadly, it was only when I learned that a young man who had visited the church had taken his life that I was convinced that I couldn't wait any longer to come out, first to my wife, lover and partner — and then also to my faith community.

— *Rev. Will McGarvey, Pastor, Community Presbyterian Church, Pittsburg, CA*

Bi-Erasure

A 2013 Pew Research study on LGBT people in the United States found that only about a quarter of those who identify as bisexual are out to the most important people in their lives. In "Why Bisexuals Stay in the Closet," (Los Angeles Times, July 14, 2013) Emily Alpert reports,

In the middle of the rainbowy revelers at the pride parade in West Hollywood, Jeremy Stacy was questioned: Are you really bisexual? "One guy came up to me and said, 'You're really gay,' said Stacy, who was standing under a sign reading "Ask a Bisexual." "I told him I had a long line of ex-girlfriends who would vehemently disagree. And he said, 'That doesn't matter, because I know you're gay.'"

Stacy had gotten the question before. From a friend who said anyone who had slept with men must be gay — even if he had also slept with women. From women who assumed he would cheat on them. From a boyfriend who insisted Stacy was really "bi now, gay later"— and dumped him when he countered he was "bi now, bi always."

Notes

1 Pew Research Center, *Survey of LGBT Americans*, http://www.pewsocialtrends.org/2013/06/13/a-survey-of-lgbt-americans, 4.

2 Jaime M. Grant, Ph.D. et al, *Injustice at Every Turn: A Report of the National Transgender Discrimination Survey*. National Center for Transgender Equality and National Gay and Lesbian Task Force, http://www.thetaskforce.org/downloads/reports/reports/ntds_full.pdf.

3 See the following:
   • Pew Research Center, *Survey of LGBT Americans*, http://www.pewsocialtrends.org/2013/06/13/a-survey-of-lgbt-americans, 4.
   • Debby Herbenick, et al. "Sexual Behavior in the United States: Results from a National Probability Sample of Men and Women Ages 14-94." *Journal of Sexual Medicine* 7s5 (2010): 255–265.
   • Anjani Chandra, PhD., William D. Mosher, PhD., and Casey Copen, PhD., *Sexual Behavior, Sexual Attraction, and Sexual Identity in the United States: Data From the 2006–2008 National Survey of Family Growth* 36 (2011).

4 Centers for Disease Control and Prevention, *Key Statistics from the National Survey of Family Growth 2006–2010*, http://www.cdc.gov/nchs/nsfg/key_statistics.htm.

5 Chandra, Mosher, and Copen, *Sexual Behavior*.

6 Ritch C. Savin-Williams and Zhana Vrangalova, *Mostly Heterosexual*, 58–88.

HEALING THE SUFFERING

Our religious traditions call on us to help heal the world. Bisexual people have suffered because of the failure of faith communities, LGBT communities, and society at large to embrace them fully. The following statistics do not indicate that being bisexual causes suffering; rather they reflect the harmful effects of discrimination, marginalization, and invisibility on bisexual persons.

Bisexual persons are at greater risk for mental health issues than lesbians, gay men, or heterosexual persons.

- Bisexual people have higher rates of mental health problems than gay men, lesbians, or straight people, including post-traumatic stress disorder[1], depression, and mood or anxiety disorders.[2]
- Bisexual people are more likely to report feeling suicidal than gay men, lesbians, or straight people.[3]
- Almost half of bisexual people have had negative experiences with mental health providers. A 2004 study of bisexual persons who accessed mental health services asked, *"What do you think is the most important issue or problem you face in being both a mental health consumer and a bisexual?"* The top response, from 42% of those in the study, was that their mental health providers invalidated or pathologized their bisexual identities by assuming that clients' bisexuality was connected to clinical issues when clients didn't agree, or assuming that bisexual attractions and behavior would disappear when clients regained psychological health.[4]

Bisexual persons have greater physical and sexual health risks than lesbians, gay men, or heterosexual persons.

- Bisexuals report higher rates of hypertension, poor or fair physical health, smoking, and alcohol use than heterosexuals, lesbians or gay men.[5, 6]
- Bisexual women in relationships with either heterosexual or lesbian partners are at greater risk of domestic violence than lesbian or heterosexual women.[7]
- Bisexual people are more likely to be victims of intimate partner violence than lesbians, gay men, or heterosexual people. Sixty-one percent of bisexual women and 37% of bisexual men report ever experiencing rape, physical violence, and/or stalking by an intimate partner (compared to 44% of lesbians, 35% of heterosexual women, 26% of gay men, and 29% of heterosexual men). Of the bisexual women who experienced intimate partner violence, approximately 90% reported that the violence was committed by an opposite sex partner.[8] Of the bisexual men who experienced intimate partner violence, 78% reported it was committed by an opposite sex partner.[9]

Bisexual persons face more stressors in daily life than lesbians, gay men, or heterosexual persons.

- In a California survey, bisexual women were more than twice as likely as lesbians to live in poverty (17.7% compared with 7.8%), and bisexual men were more likely to live in poverty than gay men (9.7% compared with 6.2%).[10]

- In a Pew Research Center survey of LGBT people in the United States, only 28% of bisexual people said that most of the important people in their life knew of their sexual orientation, compared with 71% of lesbians and 77% of gay men.[11]

- Only 22% of bisexual people in the Pew survey said that their sexual orientation was a positive factor in their lives, compared with 46% of gay men and 38% of lesbians.[12]

- A study that examined heterosexual adults' attitudes towards bisexual men and women found that "respondents' attitudes toward bisexual men and women were more negative than for all other groups except injecting drug users."[13]

Bisexual youth are at particular risk.

- According to a 2011 report from the U.S. Centers for Disease Control, the prevalence of risky health behaviors such as attempted suicide, tobacco use, alcohol use, other drug use, and behaviors that contribute to unintentional injuries and violence is higher among students who identify as bisexual or who have sexual contact with more than one sex than among heterosexual or gay/lesbian students.[14]

Questions for Reflection

1. What responsibility does our faith community have for healing the suffering of bisexual persons? What principles of our faith uphold that responsibility?

2. Would a person who identifies as bisexual feel comfortable in our faith community? Why or why not?

3. Reflect on the statistics presented in "Healing the Suffering." In what ways can our faith community ameliorate such suffering? Why is this important even if you aren't aware of congregants who identify as bisexual?

4. What are some ways in which congregations and religious leaders can create safe spaces for bisexual persons to integrate their sexuality and their faith?

Notes

1   Andrea L. Roberts et al. "Pervasive Trauma Exposure Among US Sexual Orientation Minority Adults and Risk of Posttraumatic Stress Disorder." *American Journal of Public Health* no. 100 (2010): 2433–2441.

2   San Francisco Human Rights Commission, "Bisexual Invisibility: Impacts and Recommendations," San Francisco Human Rights Commission LGBT Advisory Committee, http://sf-hrc.org/sites/sf-hrc.org/files/migrated/FileCenter/Documents/HRC_Publications/Articles/Bisexual_Invisiblity_Impacts_and_Recommendations_March_2011.pdf.

3   Ibid.

4   Emily H. Page, "Mental Health Services Experiences of Bisexual Women and Bisexual Men: An Empirical Study," *Journal Of Bisexuality* 4, no. 1–2 (2004): 137–160.

5   David J. Brennan et al. "Men's Sexual Orientation and Health in Canada," *Canadian Journal of Public Health* 101, no.3 (2010): 255–258.

6   Leah S. Steele et al. "Women's Sexual Orientation and Health: Results from a Canadian Population-Based Survey," *Women & Health* 49, no. 5 (2009): 353–367.

7   San Francisco Human Rights Commission, *Bisexual Invisibility*, http://sf-hrc.org/index.aspx?page=128#LGBT and Intersex Communities.

8   M.L. Walters et al. "The National Intimate Partner and Sexual Violence Survey (NISVS): 2010 Findings on Victimization by Sexual Orientation," National Center for Injury Prevention and Control of the Centers for Disease Control and Prevention, http://www.cdc.gov/violenceprevention/pdf/nisvs_sofindings.pdf.

9   Ibid.

10 Albelda, R. et. al. "Poverty in the Lesbian, Gay, and Bisexual Community," The Williams Institute, UCLA, quoted in *Bisexual Invisibility*, http://sf-hrc.org/index.aspx?page=128#LGBT and Intersex Communities.

11 Pew Research Center, *Survey of LGBT Americans.* http://www.pewsocialtrends.org/2013/06/13/a-survey-of-lgbt-americans/.

12 Ibid.

13 Gregory M. Herek. "Heterosexuals' Attitudes toward Bisexual Men and Women in the United States," *The Journal of Sex Research* 39, no. 4 (2002): 264–274.

14 Centers for Disease Control and Prevention, "Sexual Identity, Sex of Sexual Contacts, and Health-Risk Behaviors Among Students in Grades 9–12 — Youth Risk Behavior Surveillance, Selected Sites, United States, 2001–2009," *Morbidity and Mortality Weekly Report* 60 (2011):1. http://www.cdc.gov/mmwr/pdf/ss/ss60e0606.pdf.

RESEARCH ON BISEXUALITY

During the past two decades, there have been many scientific studies that explore the origins, or etiology, of sexual orientation. The majority of research suggests that an individual's sexual orientation is caused by a complex combination of genetics, prenatal hormones, and, perhaps, socio-cultural psychosocial factors. As society advances in its acceptance of people of various sexual orientations and gender identities, research also advances, and more will undoubtedly be learned about these subjects in the coming years. What is most clear is that there is no single factor that determines sexual orientation or gender identity.[1]

Few studies have explored the origins of sexual orientation in general and bisexuality in particular in both men and women. Most studies have looked at the etiology of homosexuality, particularly in men, rather than either the origin of bisexuality or heterosexuality. The few studies of both men and women indicate that there are significant differences in sexual orientation between them. As one researcher said, "Men seem to be more categorical in their sexual orientation; they are more likely to be either heterosexual or homosexual. Women, on the other hand, tend to be more flexible in their sexual orientation, less categorically heterosexual or homosexual."[2] Researcher Lisa Diamond contends that a more accurate way to describe flexibility in sexual orientation is that in general there appears to be a capacity for flexibility or fluidity in both men and women. In addition, she says, newer studies show that far more people have bisexual attractions than exclusively same-sex attractions.[3]

Erotic attraction is often measured in scientific studies by asking study participants to view sexually explicit films while completing surveys of their emotional responses and measuring their physiological arousal.[4] In general, men's responses while watching erotic materials correspond to their stated preferred sex, with both heterosexual and homosexual men responding at least somewhat to images of women engaging in same-sex sexual behaviors. Some straight-identified men who participated in these studies experienced response to films of two men engaging in intercourse, although it was not as strong as their response to heterosexual activities.[5]

In one study, straight women's responses varied according to the sexual activity depicted rather than the sex of the partner. The authors of this study caution that the fact "that heterosexual women's sexual responses do not distinguish between depictions of female targets or depictions of male targets does not mean heterosexual women are bisexual in orientation."[6] Another study measured bisexual interest by studying how long subjects viewed pictures of people of different sexes. The study "demonstrated the existence of a bisexual pattern of sexual interest in both bisexual men and women."[7]

In the first longitudinal study of female bisexuality, researcher Lisa M. Diamond found that evidence was not consistent with the idea that bisexuality is a transitional orientation. She writes that "bisexuality may best be interpreted as a stable pattern of attraction to both sexes in which the *specific balance* of same-sex to other-sex desires necessarily varies according to interpersonal and situational factors."[8]

There is a need to continue to study the science of sexual orientation and how it develops in people of all sexes and genders. There is also a need for greater scholarship on how gender identity intersects with sexual orientation.

For faith communities and congregations addressing bisexuality, the important point of the research to date is that bisexuality is indeed an enduring sexual orientation as real as heterosexuality and homosexuality; that it differs between men and women; and that people's self-identification and orientation may vary by relationship and over time.

Questions for Reflection

1. Reflect on the information about how men and women experience sexual orientation differently. What reasons might there be for these differences? Do you think they are cultural, biological, or a combination of both? Does it make a difference what the reason is?

2. Why are more young women currently engaging in same-sex sexual behaviors than in the past? What implications does that have for youth group programs, education, and counseling?

3. What difference might it make if a gene for bisexuality is found? What difference might it make in the acceptance of bisexual people?

4. Reflect on science and faith. How do the two complement each other in understanding bisexuality?

5. How does the science of sexuality inform your thinking and understanding about your own sexuality? About sexuality in general?

Notes

1 Palmer and Haffner, *Time to Seek.*

2 Lisa J. Cohen, PhD., "Does Sexuality Differ for Women and Men?" *Psychology Today* (2011), http://www.psychologytoday.com/blog/handy-psychology-answers/201102/does-sexuality-differ-men-and-women.

3 Dr. Lisa Diamond, (professor of Developmental and Health Psychology at the University of Utah), in discussion with the authors, March 28, 2014.

4 Also see "What Sexual Scientists Know about Gender Differences and Similarities in Sexuality," www.sexscience.org.

5 Meredith L. Chivers, et. al., "Gender and Sexual Orientation Differences in Sexual Response to Sexual Activities Versus Gender of Actors in Sexual Films," *Journal of Personality and Social Psychology* 93 no. 6 (2007): 1108–1121.

6 Ibid.

7 Megan Ebsworth and Martin L. Lalumière, "Viewing Time as a Measure of Bisexual Sexual Interest," *Archives of Sexual Behavior* 41 no. 1 (2012): 161–172.

8 Lisa M. Diamond, *Female Bisexuality* 44 no. 1, 5–14.

Part Two

SACRED TEXTS AND RELIGIOUS TRADITIONS

Support for affirming and celebrating bisexual persons in faith communities and society can be found in the overarching messages in sacred texts about love, justice, and welcome for those who are marginalized. The richness of sacred texts allows for a variety of interpretations, including those that affirm bisexual persons. Today, theologians, religious leaders and people of faith are approaching sacred texts and traditions with fresh questions and new understandings.

THEOLOGICAL CONNECTIONS

There are many faith-based arguments for activism for bisexual rights and justice. Some of the following specific theological connections may resonate with your faith community or tradition.

The Religious Institute's founding document, *The Religious Declaration on Sexual Morality, Justice, and Healing*, calls for "**a sexual ethic focused on personal relationships and social justice rather than particular sexual acts**." This overarching call for sexual justice is a helpful way to reframe discussions of sexual morality both in faith communities and in the public sphere.

Bisexuality reminds us of the **diversity, beauty, and wonder of creation**. Moving beyond the binary of gay/lesbian and straight invites people into the mystery and complexity of human sexuality. Attempting to categorize people, while a natural human instinct, limits our thinking about humanity and about the Divine. Faith communities and religious leaders can appeal to the diversity of creation when advocating for a broader understanding of sexuality.

Working for bisexual rights and justice need not be seen as taking away from other areas of sexual and social justice advocacy. Invoking the theological principle of **abundance**, religious leaders and faith communities can instead show how working for justice for any group of people enriches and informs all justice work. Oppressive systems affect the many interlocking identities and experiences of people (race, ethnicity, sexual orientation, gender identity, socioeconomic status, ability, and age, among others); justice work necessarily involves addressing multiple injustices.

Many religious traditions place a great value on **individual conscience**. The sacredness of human agency and choice can be lifted up as guiding principles in discussions of sexual orientation and gender identity. All human beings are moral agents who can discern for themselves how their faith and sexuality intersect.

Sexual justice calls on us to respect the **dignity and sacred worth of all persons**. Faith communities and religious leaders can uphold the sacred worth of bisexual people when challenging harmful myths and stereotypes and seeking to bring healing and wholeness to bisexual persons who have often been marginalized by lesbian/gay and straight communities. When advocating for bisexual visibility and rights in the public arena, upholding the dignity of all persons is essential.

Discussions about bisexuality expand the conversation about sexual orientation. Religious leaders and faith communities can use this as a starting point to remind people that **everyone has a sexual orientation**. This can help counter "us vs. them" thinking and promote unity as well as lift up shared community values.

Questions for Reflection

1. Which of these theological connections resonate most for your and your faith community? Which ones are more difficult to consider?

2. How can working for justice for bisexual persons enrich the faith community?

3. What theological principles would you add to this list?

HEBREW AND CHRISTIAN SCRIPTURES

There can be no doubt that the Hebrew and Christian Scriptures play a large role in American discourse about sexuality and lesbian, gay, bisexual, and transgender people. Most of the time, that role is to oppress or marginalize LGBT people. The challenge is to discern insights and guidance from the Scriptures that can be useful in contemporary discussions of sexuality and gender.

The Religious Institute guidebook *A Time to Seek: Study Guide on Sexual and Gender Diversity*, states that "Although the Bible has a good deal to say about sexuality, many theologians and people of faith believe that much of it does not speak to modern societies. For instance, parts of the Bible explicitly forbid certain behaviors — such as divorce, intercourse during menstruation, and re-marriage — that many faith communities now accept. Other biblical texts permit (or tacitly approve) such practices as polygamy, prostitution, and the treatment of women as property that are now prohibited. Meanwhile, the Bible is essentially silent on abortion, birth control, and masturbation."[1]

There are few biblical references to sexual diversity, and the Bible does not address current understandings about sexual orientation and gender identity, concepts that were unknown to the cultures of biblical times. There are no specific verses in the Hebrew or Christian Scriptures that explicitly address bisexuality.

Passages that reference same-sex sexual activity should be viewed in the context of what the ancient world that produced the Bible understood about sexual activity.[2] These six passages from the Bible are consistently used to marginalize lesbian, gay, and bisexual people, but current biblical scholarship effectively challenges such oppressive interpretations.

Genesis 19:1–29

The story of Sodom and Gomorrah is frequently cited as an indictment of homosexuality. However, this interpretation does not reflect the social realities of the ancient Near East or the perspective of biblical writers. The story tells how the men of Sodom sought to force the two angels visiting Lot's home outside "so that we may know them" (Genesis 19:5). The townsmen were threatening Lot's visitors with gang rape, a means of showing domination that some surrounding cultures used with their enemies. Their act was a flagrant violation of the hospitality codes of the ancient Near East. The fact that

Lot offers his two virgin daughters to satisfy the mob testifies both to the sanctity of the hospitality codes and to the cultural distance between ancient and contemporary societies. The biblical writers do not identify homosexuality as the reason for Sodom's ultimate punishment. Certain Hebrew and apocryphal texts specify the sins of Sodom as pride, arrogance, neglect of the poor, and hostility to strangers (Ezekiel 16:49, Sirach 16:8, Wisdom of Solomon 19:13–15).

Leviticus 18:22, Leviticus 20:13, Romans 1:24–27

Many theologians believe the Leviticus passages on male same-sex behavior refer to the rejection of foreign cults that practiced sacred prostitution during religious rites. The passages are part of what is known today as the "holiness code," which also called for dietary laws, circumcision and other practices. The holiness code is generally thought to have originally been intended to maintain the distinctiveness of the Jewish culture during the time of the Babylonian exile (6th century BCE). Similarly, the passage in Romans refers to various examples of idolatrous behaviors in 1st-century society. The sexual activities that Paul prohibits are most likely male adult/child sexual behavior and male prostitution, and it is uncertain what specific female sexual behavior he denounces as "unnatural." As Harvard theologian Peter J. Gomes writes, "All Paul knew of homosexuality was the debauched pagan expression of it."[3]

1 Corinthians 6:9–10, 1 Timothy 1:9–11

In the Corinthians and Timothy texts, scholars disagree about whether these texts refer to homosexual behaviors, to sexual promiscuity in general, or to temple prostitution. In the times when the Bible was written, sexual relationships were based on rigid gender roles and the concept of power and dominance. The authors of these texts had no concept of an equal, loving monogamous relationship between two people of the same sex. When the texts are read today, it is important to remember that the original authors are not referring to homosexual relationships as we understand them today nor to our modern understanding of homosexuality as a sexual orientation.[4]

I feel ambivalent about wrestling with bisexuality largely through text. While the textual tradition offers infinite inspiration, exegesis detached from diverse lived experience can objectify bisexual people. As a bisexual Jewishly-observant woman married to a man I am personally aware of how easy it is to be silent about my identity.

— *Chaplain Allison Kestenbaum, Jewish Theological Seminary*

Love and Justice

Many Jews and Christians ground their commitment to embracing the diversity of sexual orientations and gender identities in the biblical call to love and justice that permeates the Hebrew and Christian Scriptures. Christian and Jewish congregations, people of faith, and religious leaders stand on solid scriptural ground when they celebrate and welcome people of all sexual orientations and gender identities as equally beloved.

The call for justice for the poor and oppressed is one of the most prominent biblical themes, particularly among the Hebrew prophets. Among the best-known passages are Amos's plea to "let justice roll down like waters, and righteousness like an ever-flowing stream," (Amos 5:24) and Micah's question, "What does the Lord require of you but to do justice, and to love kindness, and to walk humbly with your God?" (Micah 6:8).

The gospels record Jesus's overarching concern for justice as well. In the gospel of Matthew, he says that those who visit prisoners, provide clothing to those who need it, care for the sick, and welcome strangers will "inherit the kingdom" (Matthew 25:34–40). The parable of the Good Samaritan in Luke 10:29–37 highlights the importance that Jesus placed on caring for others, even those who were considered different or outsiders.

The overarching message of the Bible is of God's love for humanity. That extravagant love, recorded in the Hebrew Scriptures and the New Testament, is a message of hope to people of all sexual orientations and gender identities.

HEBREW SCRIPTURES

Many passages in the Hebrew Scriptures offer messages of hope and healing to bisexual persons, like the biblical affirmation that *all* humans are created in God's image.

"Humankind was created as God's reflection: in the divine image God created them..." (Genesis 1:27a).[5]

This passage conveys an expansive message: that all of humanity — in all of our glorious diversity — is created in God's image. If God is sacred and divine, then all people are likewise sacred and divine, each having inherent value and worth. (Similar passages occur in Genesis 5:1–3, Genesis 9:6, 1 Corinthians: 11:7, and James 3:9, among others.)

In a column she wrote for The Huffington Post, out bisexual Presbyterian minister Rev. Dr. Janet Edwards reflects on this verse from Jeremiah 1:5, "Before I formed you in the womb I knew you." She says, "God knew me and loved me before I was even formed. God chose to make me bisexual. And God wants me to live a life in harmony with the laws Jesus gave to us."[6]

The command that "you shall love your neighbor as yourself" appears in the Hebrew Scriptures (Leviticus 19:18) and is quoted by Jesus in all three synoptic gospels (Matthew 22:39, Mark 12:31, Luke 10:27). This command sums up a central theme of both the Hebrew Bible and the New Testament: that love is the guiding principle of ethical living and right relationship with others.

Biblical scholars have pointed to the relationships between Jonathan and David (recounted in 1 and 2 Samuel) and between Ruth and Naomi (recounted in the book of Ruth) as examples of same-sex loving relationships. Some theologians have identified these relationships as gay or lesbian.[6] However, in both Biblical accounts, the people involved might today be identified as bisexual, at least in their emotional attractions, as these two stories portray men and women in significant relationships with people of different sexes.[7]

Jonathan, David, and David's Wives and Concubines

The biblical story of Jonathan and David depicts men who, in today's terms, might be described as having a bisexual orientation. David is described as being in a covenanted relationship with Jonathan, and he is also reported to have had at least seven wives (1 Chronicles 3:1–9) and numerous concubines (2 Samuel 5:13).

Jonathan first encounters David after David has killed a Philistine giant (Goliath) for Jonathan's father, King Saul. A passage from 1 Samuel recounts that at their first meeting, "the souls of Jonathan and David became intertwined, and Jonathan loved David with all his heart" (1 Samuel 18:1). Later, the book of 1 Samuel recounts how King Saul sought to put David to death, as his prowess as a warrior was a threat to Saul's kingship. However, more than once, Jonathan warned David of his father's intentions, allowing David to escape from Saul. The text repeatedly mentions the covenant or pledge of love between the two men.

- "Then Jonathan made a covenant with David, because he loved him as his own soul" (1 Samuel 18:3).
- "Jonathan made David swear again by his love for him; for he loved him as he loved his own life" (1 Samuel 20:17).
- "Then Jonathan said to David, 'Go in peace, since both of us have sworn in the name of the Lord, saying, 'The Lord shall be between me and you, and between my descendants and your descendants, forever'" (1 Samuel 20:42a).

David's lament at Jonathan's death is recorded in 2 Samuel 1:26:

> I am distressed for you, my brother Jonathan;
> greatly beloved were you to me;
> your love to me was wonderful,
> passing the love of women.

While the story of Jonathan depicts David in a covenanted and loving relationship with a man, the story of Bathsheba, who became David's seventh wife, leaves no room for doubt that David was attracted to women as well:

> It happened, late one afternoon, when David rose from his couch and was walking about on the roof of the king's house, that he saw from the roof a woman bathing; the woman was very beautiful. David sent someone to inquire about the woman. It was reported, 'This is Bathsheba, daughter of Eliam, the wife of Uriah the Hittite.' So David sent messengers to fetch her, and she came to him, and he lay with her (2 Samuel 11:2-4).

Ruth and Naomi

The story recounted in the biblical book of Ruth tells of two women who had meaningful intimate relationships with other and same-sex partners. Naomi and Ruth are each married to men at the beginning of the story, Naomi to Elimilech and Ruth to Naomi's son Mahon. When both men die, Naomi resolves to go back to her homeland of Judah and encourages Ruth to return to hers. Since Ruth has no sons (which would bind her to Naomi in the culture of the time), this is the expected course of action.

However, Ruth refuses to go back to her homeland, and the feelings that she expresses toward her mother-in-law Naomi parallel the feelings expressed in biblical relationships that are primary attachments. Ruth 1:14b says, "Orpah kissed her mother-in-law, but Ruth clung to her." "Clung to" is the same Hebrew word (*dabaq*) used to describe a marriage relationship in Genesis 2:24: "Therefore a man leaves his father and his mother and clings to his wife, and they become one flesh." Although there is no indication in the text that the women were erotically involved, it is very clear that they are involved in a primary emotional relationship. While some theologians have written that Ruth and Naomi are in a same-sex relationship, it is more accurate to describe them as women with primary relationships with both men and women.

In a lyrical passage used in many marriage ceremonies today (and also used in Jewish conversion rites), Ruth vows to return with Naomi to Bethlehem in Judah:

> Where you go, I will go;
>   where you lodge, I will lodge;
> your people shall be my people,
>   and your God my God.
> Where you die, I will die—
>   there will I be buried.
> May the Lord do thus and so to me,
>   and more as well,
> if even death parts me from you! (Ruth 1:16b–17)

Ruth and Naomi settle in Bethlehem, and eventually Ruth remarries a man named Boaz, because he is a relative of Naomi's and her "redeemer-trustee" (a male relative charged with making sure that his widowed kinswoman, Naomi, is protected). Ruth has a son, Obed, with Boaz and the text says that Naomi became the child's nurse (Ruth 4:16). The women of the neighborhood are said to have rejoiced that "A son has been born to Naomi" (Ruth 4:17). The implication is that Ruth had the child for Naomi, and that Ruth and Naomi raised Obed together.

It takes both couples (Ruth and Naomi, and Ruth and Boaz) to produce and raise this child, who represents the hope and future of the Davidic lineage. Obed and Ruth are also named in the Gospel of Matthew's extended genealogy of Jesus, where Ruth is one of only five women mentioned.[8]

Modern understandings of sexual orientation cannot be found in the Hebrew Scriptures. These texts date from thousands of years ago and are products of a culture that is radically different from our own culture. However, the behaviors and feelings that are depicted in these stories, and the fact that they are presented without commentary, points to a society that may have been more accepting of diverse intimate relationships than many people assume.

A REFLECTION ON SONG OF SONGS (*SHIR HASHIRIM*):

Shir HaShirim, one of the most lyrical books of the Jewish canon and a beautiful love song has an unusual voicing. The gender of the beloved changes through the book, sometimes male, sometimes female. One doesn't always know the gender of the speaker, leaving open a reading that the love that is being spoken could be same gender love.

Given that this book is framed as both a love song between humans and a love song between G-d and Israel, and given that the traditional view of G-d in Judaism is that G-d is both male and female and everything in between and outside of those categories, *Shir HaShirim* stands as a testament to love beyond gender.

Having readers of various genders read out the text on Shabbat during the intermediate days of Passover, when it is traditional to read the text, offers welcome, affirmation and consciousness raising, not to mention amplifying the message of boundless eternal love.

— *Rabbi Debra Kolodny, Executive Director, Nehirim*

THE NEW TESTAMENT

Jesus

Biblical scholars have pointed out that, "the Jesus of the Gospels nowhere makes any explicit statement about homosexuality in general, nor even the homosexual practices that might have been commonly recognized in his day."[9] In the Greco-Roman world of Jesus's time, same-sex sexual behaviors did not preclude other-sex sexual behaviors. Indeed, according to one scholar, "What we today call bisexuality was far more the expected pattern of behavior."[10]

For example, some biblical scholars believe that in the context of Greco-Roman society, the biblical story of the centurion and his "servant" that appears in three of the four gospels[11] is about two people in a same-sex sexual relationship.[12] They point out that Jesus makes no mention of this when he heals the servant. Instead, he holds up the centurion as a model of faith, saying, "Truly I tell you, in no one in Israel have I found such faith" (Matthew 8:10b). And while these biblical scholars note that the "servant" is most likely the centurion's lover, few if any mention that the centurion is also probably married to a woman, as would have been the norm in the Greco-Roman culture.

Jesus promotes alternative family structures in many gospel stories. For example, in Mark 3:31–35 (see also Matthew 12:46–50), Jesus asks, "Who are my mother and my brothers?" and answers, "Whoever does the will of God is my brother and sister and mother." And in Luke 14:26, he says, "Whoever comes to me and does not hate father and mother, wife and children, brothers and sisters, yes, and even life itself, cannot be my disciple." These passages make it clear that Jesus does not privilege "traditional" family structures among his followers. Indeed, his disciples in the gospel accounts are men who have chosen to ignore societal roles as married men and fathers and instead follow Jesus and participate in his ministry.

Jesus embraces sexual minorities as well. For example, he makes what seems to be a perplexing statement about eunuchs in Matthew 19:10–12: "His disciples said to him, 'If such is the case of a man with his wife, it is better not to marry.' But he said to them, 'Not everyone can accept this teaching, but only those to whom it is given. For there are eunuchs who have been so from birth, and there are eunuchs who have been made eunuchs by others, and there are eunuchs who have made themselves eunuchs for the sake of the kingdom of heaven. Let anyone accept this who can.'" Jesus appears to acknowledge that there are sexual minorities (the word "eunuch" may not have been literal in this passage) who were so from birth. The Rev. Dr. Theodore Jennings, Jr., professor of biblical and constructive theology at Chicago Theological Seminary, argues that the saying about eunuchs is consistent with Matthew's concern for the sexually marginalized throughout his gospel account.[14]

The gospel accounts of Jesus's life indicate that sex, gender, and norms about sexuality mattered little to him. Jesus healed women deemed "sexually impure" (Matthew 9:20–22, Mark 5:25-34, Luke 8:43-48), allowed a prostitute to anoint his feet (Matthew 26:6–13, Mark 14:3–9, Luke 7:37–50, John 12:1–8), and defended a woman who committed adultery (John 8:2–11). He had important emotional connections with men and women: Mary of Bethany (Martha's sister), Lazarus, Mary Magdalene, and the "beloved disciple," for example.

Paul

The letters from Paul (as well as those attributed to Paul) that are included in the Christian canon record much about the struggles of the early communities of Jesus's followers. Paul's main concern was creating and maintaining stable communities that avoided harassment by civil and religious authorities. Because of this, many parts of his letters conform to the norms of the day and contradict the more radical and egalitarian actions and teachings of Jesus as recorded in the gospels. (See 1 Corinthians 7, 1 Corinthians 14:34–35, and Romans 1:24–27.) However, texts of liberation and hope can also be found in Paul's writings.

In the book of Galatians, Paul records what scholars believe to be a fragment of an early baptismal liturgy. In it, there is a vision of the world to come in which the many binary categories assigned to humanity no longer exist: "There is no longer Jew or Greek, there is no longer slave or free, there is no longer male and female; for all of you are one in Christ Jesus" (Galatians 3:28).

This is an especially powerful passage for bisexual people who are marginalized by binary thinking that seeks to restrict their attractions, behaviors, and emotions to one of two sexes. Paul's proclamation that becoming one in Christ Jesus erases the distinctions between males and females also celebrates sexual and gender identities that erase or transcend these distinctions. As author, theologian, and Metropolitan Community Church minister the Rev. Chris Glaser has written, "If there is no longer male and female in Christ Jesus, it does not matter to God which gender we love, which gender we are, or which gender we believe ourselves to be."[15]

In an often-quoted passage in the book of Romans, Paul affirms that nothing, most especially not a person's identity, can come between humanity and God's love: "For I am convinced that neither death, nor life, nor angels, nor rulers, nor things present, nor things to come, nor powers, nor height, nor depth, nor anything else in all creation, will be able to separate us from the love of God in Christ Jesus our Lord" (Romans 8:38–39).

Questions for Reflection

1. What is your reaction to considering the biblical accounts of David and Jonathan, Ruth and Naomi, the healing of the centurion's "servant," and the accounts of eunuchs through the lens of bisexuality?

2. How can we understand passages that many people believe condemn non-heterosexual behaviors in light of the overall scriptural messages of "love your neighbor as yourself" and the message that "all are created in God's image"?

3. Which of the scriptural interpretations above resonate most for you and your faith community? Which ones might be more difficult to consider?

4. Are particular sexual acts moral or sinful in and of themselves, or do they need to be judged in the context of relationship? What does it mean that the *Religious Declaration on Sexual Morality, Justice, and Healing* (see inside front cover) calls for a "sexual ethic based on personal relationship and social justice rather than particular sexual acts"?

Notes

1 Palmer and Haffner, *Time to Seek*.

2 Rev. Mona West, PhD., *The Bible and Homosexuality*, Metropolitan Community Churches, http://mccchurch.org/resources/mcc-theologies/.

3 Peter Gomes, *The Good Book: Reading the Bible with Mind and Heart*, (New York: William Morrow and Company, 1996), 158.

4 The section on the six "clobber passages" is quoted from Palmer and Haffner, *A Time to Seek*, 27–28.

5 Priests for Equality, *The Inclusive Bible* (Lanham, Maryland: Rowman & Littlefield, 2007).

6 Rev. Dr. Janet Edwards, "Top Five Questions Asked About Being A Bisexual Minister," *The Huffington Post*, 2012, http://www.huffingtonpost.com/rev-dr-janet-edwards/top-five-questions-asked-about-being-a-bisexual-minister_b_1280433.html.

7 Also see Theodore W. Jennings, Jr., *Jacob's Wound* (New York: T & T Clark International, 2005), 227–233.

8 Rev. Dr. Janet Edwards, "Top Five Questions Asked About Being A Bisexual Minister," *The Huffington Post*, 2012, http://www.huffingtonpost.com/rev-dr-janet-edwards/top-five-questions-asked-about-being-a-bisexual-minister_b_1280433.html.

9 Matthew 1:1, 2a, 5b

10 Deryn Guest et al. eds., *The Queer Bible Commentary*, (London: SCM Press, 2006), 16. See also: John Boswell, *Christianity, Social Tolerance, and Homosexuality* (Chicago: The University of Chicago Press, 1980), 91–117 and Kelly Brown Douglas, *Sexuality and the Black Church*, (Maryknoll, New York: Orbis Books, 1999), 89–91.

11 Deryn Guest et al. eds., *The Queer Bible Commentary*, (London: SCM Press, 2006), 152.

12 Matthew 8:5–13, Luke 7:1–10, and John 4:46–54.

13 Guest et al, *Queer Bible Commentary*, 537–538.

14 Theodore W. Jennings, Jr., *The Man Jesus Loved* (Cleveland: The Pilgrim Press, 2003), 150.

15 Chris Glaser, *The Word is Out* (Harper, San Francisco: 1994) 10/3.

PERSPECTIVES FROM RELIGIOUS TRADITIONS

While most people today do not rely on religious texts and tradition for scientific or sociological understandings of sexual identity, theological reflection on sexuality is an important task for people of faith. In this section, theologians from different traditions were invited to offer their faith tradition's perspectives on bisexuality.

ONE IMAM'S PERSPECTIVE ON BISEXUALITY
by Imam Daayiee Abdullah, Muslims for Progressive Values

A progressive reading of the Quran promotes the affirmation of all Muslims, regardless of sexual orientation, gender identity, sex, or other demographics. One surat (chapter) in Al-Rum, 30:22, provides a clear indicator that God created humanity with a great diversity of language, colors, tastes and styles and temperaments: "And of His signs is the creation of the heavens and the earth and the diversity of your languages and your colors. Indeed in that are signs for those of knowledge." It follows that God created all people as equals and that the equality of justice, compassion and mercy for all of God's creation is expansive both externally by what we see and internally by what we sense and know intuitively. This understanding promotes a unity among our diverse Muslim community.

My interpretation of the Quran is based on a wide array of modern Islamic scholars, such as Fazlur Rahman, Khalid M. Abou El-Fadl, Dr. Taha Jabir Al-Alawani, Mahmoud Mohamed Taha, and Abdullahi Ahmed An-Na'im, who are aware of interpretations that affirm the diversity of sexual minorities within Islamic culture. Their work provides a basis from which to glean insights that are relevant for our understanding of bisexuality.

In her book *Inside the Gender Jihad*, Dr. Amina Wadud, an American Islamic scholar, has reframed the historical patriarchal view of the creation of humanity with God at the top, followed by men, women, and finally sexual minorities, into a more inclusive view of humanity. She proposed a shape more like a triangle than a vertical line, with God at the top and males and females at the other two points, on an equal plane. This view of God and humanity promotes the equality that Dr. Wadud believes is found in the overall intent of the Quran.[1]

This conception of humanity and God can be expanded to include sexual diversity that is expressed on the spectrum between male and female and between masculine and feminine. In this model, all sexual orientations and gender identities, including bisexuality, are equal under God.

A BLACK CHURCH PERSPECTIVE ON BISEXUALITY
by Rev. Dr. Kelly Brown Douglas, professor and chair of Religion, Goucher College

The designation "Black Church" does not point to a singular institution or faith community. Instead, the "Black Church" refers to a disparate grouping of churches that reflect the diversity of the black community itself. These churches are diversified by origin, denomination, doctrine, worshipping culture, spiritual expression, class, size and other less obvious factors. Yet, as disparate as black churches are, they do share a common history and play a unique role in black life, both of which attest to their collective identity as the Black Church. Moreover, the Black Church remains one of the most significant influences upon black values, especially those about sexuality.

Because the term "Black Church" encompasses such a diverse community, there is not a monolithic position in terms of its beliefs or attitudes toward issues of sexuality in general or bisexuality in particular. While there are prevailing attitudes that characterize the Black Church community, such as attitudes toward LGBTQ sexual identities, there are also noteworthy exceptions to these attitudes. With that caveat, the following are some general observations on bisexuality in the Black Church.

Sexuality as a whole remains virtually a taboo issue within the Black Church community. Historical narratives which caricature black people as hyper-sexualized beings have combined with evangelical Protestant narratives which proclaim non-procreative sexuality to be sinful to foster a "puritanical" intransigence on sexual matters within the black faith community. Thus, the Apostle Paul's dictum that "it is better to marry than to burn with passion" remains a prevailing attitude within the Black Church community. Sexuality is viewed as a necessary but undesirable part of the human condition. Such an attitude not only makes it virtually impossible to have frank discussions about matters of sexuality, it also means that lesbian/gay sexual expressions are considered sinful because they are considered non-procreative.

This narrow view of sexuality has several implications for bisexuality within the Black Church community.

- First, the notion that one can be bisexual suggests that there is some ability to make a choice about one's sexual orientation. In this regard, bisexuality is not seen as a valid sexual identity. Rather, it is seen as a state of confusion at best, with one having the ability to make the choice to be "heterosexual." That one would choose to be bisexual would mean one is choosing a sinful lifestyle.

- Second, that bisexuality is an option serves to further marginalize if not demonize lesbian and gay persons for whom it is not. In this regard, bisexuality becomes the lesser of two sins as it provides once again at least the possibility of "conversion" to "straight" identity.

- Third, within a church community where gender identification is also sexualized, bisexuality threatens notions of masculinity and femininity. What it means to be female is defined in relation to a male and vice versa. Bisexuality challenges the sexualized gender binary within the black faith community, thus rendering it an even more difficult identity to affirm.

- Finally, it is perhaps bisexuality that challenges most directly Black Church attitudes toward gender and sexuality. Bisexuality defies dualistic either/or notions of sexuality, disrupts socially constructed notions of gender, and points to the dynamic and fluid nature of human sexuality.

It is in engaging in sexual discourse and in recognizing bisexual identities that the Black Church community will be able to move forward in appreciating the richness of human sexuality in general.

EXPANDING OUR COVENANTS: BISEXUALITY AND THE JEWISH COMMUNITY

by Chaplain Allison Kestenbaum, Jewish Theological Seminary

As is often the case in Judaism, a richly exegetical tradition, various authorities draw on biblical texts and subsequent commentaries to offer perspectives about the status of LGBT individuals, their place and spiritual rights within the religious community. These, in addition to statements issued by several denominations and organizations, offer a broad array of viewpoints.

Many contemporary Jewish statements about LGBT individuals are vague or absent regarding bisexual identity. Those that are more explicit deal with one limited aspect of bisexual identity — same-sex sexual behaviors — rather than about the complex topics of sexual attraction or orientation. It is rarely acknowledged in these statements that bisexuality represents an identity that complicates previous understandings of sexual identity and orientation as one of two polarities — "gay" or "straight" — and what this means in Jewish tradition that privileges heterosexual relationships.

The rainbow is an image from the Torah which can offer encouragement to individuals who are stepping forward and into communities that grapple with understanding bisexuality. The rainbow is also an emblem of LGBT pride and safe haven around the world. In the Jewish tradition, the rainbow is a sign of the covenant between God and humanity. The rainbow represents an enhanced and more nuanced covenant between God and human beings. In Genesis, God makes two covenants. The first is before the flood: God promises a place in the ark, and continued survival, to Noah and his family

(6:18). After the flood God makes a second covenant, accompanied by the rainbow as a visual sign and broadening of the promise to all of humanity going forward (7:21–22).

Just as God was capable of and willing to extend the covenant as more information about the vast and complicated nature of humanity came to light, so too can Jewish communities amend, deepen and offer more visible covenant to those who identify as Jewish and bisexual. Sexuality, much like the rainbow, can be visible but is never fully concrete. Achieving greater visibility of bisexuality may feel arduous to those who have already worked hard to stretch their bounds of understanding about sexuality. Bisexual individuals themselves, many of whom are perceived as either gay or straight, may question why it is worthwhile to come out in their religious communities. But in doing all of this, humanity is following a divine example of making a visible covenant. God realized that human beings, by our very nature, do better when there is visibility. So too does greater visibility of bisexuality lead to an ever-widening covenant with the diversity of sexual orientation and the array of how each individual expresses identity.

PASSING AS A PROTESTANT
by Rev. Will McGarvey, pastor of Community Presbyterian Church of Pittsburg, CA

Let's admit that not all Christians agree on what the Bible means, nor how it speaks into our modern world. It is natural for people to focus on only one of the many metaphors in the Bible because it fits their particular cosmology. Sadly, some people are heavily invested in a dualistic, cause-and-effect worldview and therefore have a Deuteronomic faith that focuses more on right and wrong, rules and punishment, and who is in and who is out that has led to the culture wars Americans have endured for the last century. The multiple authors of Deuteronomy together espoused a cause and effect theology that essentially says: If you follow the law, you will be blessed. If you don't, you will be punished. Some Christians still live by this code, which other parts of the Bible speak against as being overly simplistic (such as Job and the majority of the book of Psalms).

What if the ancients were wrong about gender identity and sexual orientation? What if our English translations aren't the best way into understanding an ancient culture's understanding of human sexuality? For those who choose only a God of cause and effect, the cost they pay is being able to describe God fully as a God of love. Can God be both a puppet-master and gracious? Philosophers for ages have pointed out that one must ultimately choose one or the other view of God.

Furthermore, the Bible in its original languages uses both feminine and masculine terminology for God. A part of reclaiming a progressive, well-considered view of the Divine is understanding the context in which God is described in the Bible and then reminding ourselves that our faith is more alive within the Ultimate than any attempt to describe it. Attempting to enforce pre-modern conceptions of God on post-modern peoples is both an insult to our intelligence and an offense to the ineffability of our experience of the Divine. Who are we to say that God hasn't changed Her mind and publically come out to accept all Her children? If the majority of humanity is bisexual, pansexual or find themselves romantically or physically attracted to multiple gender expressions, who are we to say that the God who created humanity with such diversity cannot love each and every part of that diversity as well?

We follow a Teacher/Master/Lord who laid his life down for others. Instead of begging, we need to show the Church another way. The Church is forever in need of losing our place of privilege in the world and we can remind the Church that it's not up to them to accept or reject us. We are Christ's own beloved children and we need to start acting like it. We can live into God's calling without asking what it will cost the institutional Church because honesty should never be the cost of membership in the Church. This is what our youth and young adults are waiting to hear and see. If we won't follow our own convictions, why should they?

A ROMAN CATHOLIC PERSPECTIVE ON BISEXUALITY

by Dr. Kate Ott, moral theologian and professor of Christian Social Ethics, Drew Theological School

Recent shifts in Roman Catholic sexual ethics have focused on revisiting how sexuality is defined and the values necessary to promote morally good relationships rather than a myopic reliance on genital acts. Various Roman Catholic Church documents speak to a broader understanding of sexuality and the sexual person. For example, the Congregation for Catholic Education teaches that sexuality is an important component of one's personality that has spiritual, biological, and psychological aspects. One's sexual orientation then is part of an individual's unique personality which shapes sexual desires and attractions 'natural' to that person. The Roman Catholic hierarchy has recognized this related to heterosexual and homosexual orientations. The Catechism states that "Everyone, man and woman, should acknowledge and accept his [sic] sexual identity" (2333). In addition, those individuals identifying as homosexual are to "be accepted with respect, compassion, and sensitivity. Every sign of unjust discrimination in their regard should be avoided" (2358).

Correlations can be made to expand the concept of sexual orientation as a 'natural' part of one's createdness to include bisexuality as an orientation or perhaps even more accurately to consider each individual as having an orientation that is as unique as their personality. Pope Francis was recently asked if he approved of homosexuality. His response supports the Catechism, as he said, "Tell me: when God looks at a gay person, does he endorse the existence of this person with love, or reject and condemn this person?...In life, God accompanies persons, and we must accompany them, starting from their situation."[2] Although the Catechism also refers to homosexual acts, unfortunately, as 'intrinsically disordered,' I have hope that the Church will continue to re-examine this issue in light of a more loving, inclusive tradition.

In light of a more robust understanding of sexuality and orientation, Todd Salzman and Michael Lawler in their book *The Sexual Person: Toward a Renewed Catholic Anthropology*, suggest the concept of holistic complementarity as a replacement for heterogenital (penis/vagina) or reproductive (openness to procreation) complementarity. Holistic complementarity recognizes that sexual relationships require orientational, physical, affective, personal, and spiritual compatibility in order to draw persons into relationship and promote flourishing of each person's sexual self. Also required for a relationship are ethical values such as justice and love; virtues which guide the relationship toward growth and prevent harm. Regardless of expanded understandings of orientation, the Roman Catholic teaching that human sexual relationships are to be monogamous and committed in order to fully live into ethical values for human well-being has not changed.

Questions for Reflection

1. What common themes exist among the different religious traditions' perspectives presented in this section?

2. What new insights can be found in traditions that are different from your own?

3. If your tradition is represented in the pieces in this section, what are your thoughts on the author's views on bisexuality? What might you add or change?

4. What in your own tradition supports a commitment to affirming bisexual persons in faith communities and society?

Notes

1 Dr. Amina Wadud, *Inside the Gender Jihad: Women's Reform in Islam*, (Oxford: Oneworld, 2006), 46–48.

2 Antonio Spadaro, SJ, "A Big Heart Open to God," interview with Pope Francis, *America: The National Catholic Review*, September 30, 2013, http://www.americamagazine.org/pope-interview.

DENOMINATIONAL STATEMENTS ON BISEXUALITY

Several religious denominations and movements have resolutions or statements calling for an end to discrimination against lesbian, gay, bisexual, and transgender persons in society; however, very few of these resolutions explicitly demonstrate an understanding of the unique concerns of bisexual persons. Most of these policies and statements address such subjects as same-sex marriage or ordination of homosexual persons. In denominational policies on LGBT issues, bisexual persons usually remain invisible. Denomination statements that specifically address bisexuality are included below.

CONSERVATIVE JEWISH MOVEMENT[1]

In 2014, The Jewish Theological Seminary (JTS), which primarily serves the Conservative Movement, expanded its discrimination and inclusion policies to include people of all sexual orientations (including bisexuals) and gender identities. The new policy reads:

Discriminatory treatment, insensitive or derogatory language or actions based on factors as such as an individual's actual or perceived race, color, national origin, ancestry, gender, religion, age, disability, sexual orientation, gender identity or expression, or other categories protected by law, are offensive and prohibited at JTS. Behavior which involves discriminatory treatment can be considered demeaning, coercive or depending upon the circumstances, threatening and intimidating. This policy applies to students and employees of JTS, as well as persons seeking status as a student or employee at JTS, except that only Jews are eligible for admission to the Rabbinical and Cantorial Schools.[2]

REFORM JUDAISM

Women of Reform Judaism, an affiliate of the Union of Reform Judaism, is the collective voice and presence of women in Reform Jewish congregational life. In 2003, Women of Reform Judaism issued a call for civil rights for bisexual and transgender persons.

Women of Reform Judaism has a longstanding history of support for human and civil rights. The organization has fought discrimination against minorities and women, and has sought equal rights for all. Since 1965 WRJ has taken specific stands in behalf of the civil rights of gay men and lesbian women.

In the last several years, transgender and bisexual communities in North America have brought their issues to the attention of advocacy groups regarding workplace discrimination and hate crimes. Moreover, because of lack of knowledge about the transgender community's unique needs and concerns, its members are discriminated against in health care and insurance coverage and in access to police, paramedic, and other emergency services and well as in public facilities. The community is also stigmatized, not accepted, and frequently ignored. Our tradition tells that all humans are created in God's image b'tselem Elohim, mandating us to relate to others with respect and to work to eliminate discrimination and hate-based acts.

In accordance with our history of strong human rights and civil rights resolutions, our policy of acceptance of all women in our congregations, and with particular reference to The Rights of Gay Men and Lesbian Women (1991), Women of Reform Judaism accordingly:

1. Calls for civil rights protections from all forms of discrimination against bisexual and transgender individuals;

2. Urges that such legislation allows transgender individuals to be seen under the law as the gender by which they identify; and

3. Calls upon sisterhoods to hold informative programs about the transgender and bisexual communities.[3]

UNITARIAN UNIVERSALIST ASSOCIATION

In 1970, the Unitarian Universalist Association's (UUA) General Assembly passed a General Resolution on "Discrimination Against Homosexuals and Bisexuals," which consistently names both homosexuals and bisexuals throughout its text. This resolution became the foundation for the denomination's long-standing affirmation of LGBT people.

Discrimination Against Homosexuals and Bisexuals: 1970 General Resolution

RECOGNIZING THAT:

1. A significant minority in this country are either homosexual or bisexual in their feelings and/or behavior;

2. Homosexuality has been the target of severe discrimination by society and in particular by the police and other arms of government;

3. A growing number of authorities on the subject now see homosexuality as an inevitable sociological phenomenon and not as a mental illness;

4. There are Unitarian Universalists, clergy and laity, who are homosexuals or bisexuals;

THEREFORE BE IT RESOLVED: That the 1970 General Assembly of the Unitarian Universalist Association:

1. Urges all peoples immediately to bring an end to all discrimination against homosexuals, homosexuality, bisexuals, and bisexuality, with specific immediate attention to the following issues:

   a. private consensual behavior between persons over the age of consent shall be the business only of those persons and not subject to legal regulations;

   b. a person's sexual orientation or practice shall not be a factor in the granting or renewing of federal security clearance, visas, and the granting of citizenship or employment;

2. Calls upon the UUA and its member churches, fellowships, and organizations immediately to end all discrimination against homosexuals in employment practices, expending special effort to assist homosexuals to find employment in our midst consistent with their abilities and desires;

3. Urges all churches and fellowships, in keeping with changing social patterns, to initiate meaningful programs of sex education aimed at providing more open and healthier understanding of sexuality in all parts of the United States and Canada, and with the particular aim to end all discrimination against homosexuals and bisexuals.[4]

Since 1970, the UUA has passed more than 15 resolutions that explicitly name bisexual people along with gay, lesbian, and/or transgender people, including a 1980 business resolution calling for "full assistance in the settlement of qualified openly gay, lesbian, and bisexual religious leaders"[5] and a 2010 business resolution ("Confronting Sexual Orientation and Gender Identity Discrimination") that resolved:

THEREFORE BE IT RESOLVED that the 2010 General Assembly affirms its commitment to the inherent worth and dignity of every human being, including lesbian, gay, bisexual and transgender individuals; and

BE IT FURTHER RESOLVED that we express this spiritual value through our employment practices, educational efforts, congregational life, public witness, and immediate advocacy for the passage of the inclusive Employment Non-Discrimination Act; and

BE IT FURTHER RESOLVED that we encourage member congregations and societies to act within their congregations and communities to promote and educate the importance of employment equality for lesbian, gay, bisexual, and transgender individuals.[6]

UNITED CHURCH OF CHRIST

At its eighteenth General Synod in 1991, the United Church of Christ adopted its "Resolution on Affirming Gay, Lesbian, and Bisexual Persons and their Ministries," which consistently names "bisexual persons" throughout its text.

Resolution on Affirming Gay, Lesbian and Bisexual Persons and Their Ministries

Whereas, in the words of the Apostle Paul, we know that "the whole creation has been groaning in travail" and we, too, feel these pains as we struggle to grow in our understanding of human sexuality;

Whereas, the actions of General Synods 10, 11, 14, 15, 16, and 17 have supported human rights of all persons in church and society, regardless of sexual orientation;

Whereas, lesbian, gay, bisexual persons and their families have shared their gifts for ministry throughout the church, and through their stories and ministries the United Church of Christ has come to a deeper understanding of the diversity of God's creation and the inclusiveness of God's call;

Therefore, Be It Resolved, the Eighteenth General Synod boldly affirms, celebrates and embraces the gifts for ministry of lesbian, gay and bisexual persons, and faithfully continues to work for justice in our church and society:

Calls upon local churches, Associations and Conferences to adopt an Open and Affirming policy. (i.e. a non-discrimination policy and a covenant of openness and affirmation of persons of lesbian, gay and bisexual orientation within the community of faith. CF: Fifteenth General Synod, 1985.)

Urgently calls upon local churches, Associations, Conferences to engage in a disciplined dialogue in which the biblical and theological foundation for congregations to be open and affirming of gay, lesbian, and bisexual persons are prayerfully discussed in light of the teachings of Jesus Christ and our Christian vocation to live as communities of grace and reconciliation. The Instrumentalities are requested to provide study resources for the United Church of Christ.

Calls upon local churches, Associations and Conferences to extend their welcome and support to openly lesbian, gay and bisexual students in-care, and to facilitate the ordination and placement of qualified lesbian, gay and bisexual candidates.

Invites all persons of the United Church of Christ to experience the struggle and joy of the journey towards openness and affirmation of all lesbian, gay and bisexual persons as children of God in the community of faith.[7]

Denominational Support for LGBT Full Inclusion

The following religious traditions have policies that support full inclusion of lesbian and gay persons, including ordination and marriage for same-sex couples:

- Central Conference of American Rabbis / Union for Reform Judaism
- Metropolitan Community Churches
- Reconstructionist Rabbinical Association / Jewish Reconstructionist Federation
- Unitarian Universalist Association
- United Church of Christ
- Unity Fellowship Churches

The following denominations and movements ordain openly lesbian, gay and bisexual clergy members:

- Conservative Judaism*
- Episcopal Church USA*
- Evangelical Lutheran Church in America
- Jewish Reconstructionist Communities
- Metropolitan Community Churches*
- Presbyterian Church (U.S.A.)*
- Reform Judaism*
- Unitarian Universalist Association*
- United Church of Christ*
- Unity Fellowship Churches

* Also ordains openly transgender clergy.

Notes

1 In 2006, the Conservative Movement's Committee on Jewish Law and Standards, published its official position permitting openly gay and lesbian students to attend Conservative seminaries. It can be read at http://www.rabbinicalassembly.org/sites/default/files/public/halakhah/teshuvot/20052010/dorff_nevins_reisner_dignity.pdf.

2 Jewish Theological Seminary, http://www.jtsa.edu/About_JTS/Administration/Policies/Discrimination_and_Sexual_Harassment.xml

3 Women of Reform Judaism, "Transgender and Bisexual Rights — 2003," http://wrj.org/Advocacy/ResolutionsStatements/ResolutionsArchive/Resolutions20002009/Resolutions2003/2003TransgenderandBisexualRights.aspx.

4 Unitarian Universalist Association, "Discrimination Against Homosexuals and Bisexuals 1970 General Resolution," http://www.uua.org/statements/statements/14482.shtml.

5 Ibid., http://www.uua.org/statements/statements/20226.shtml.

6 Unitarian Universalist Association, "Confronting Sexual Orientation and Gender Identity Discrimination 2010 Business Resolution," http://www.uua.org/statements/statements/169267.shtml.

7 United Church of Christ, "Resolution on Affirming Gay, Lesbian, and Bisexualpersons and Their Ministries," http://www.ucc.org/assets/pdfs/1991-RESOLUTION-ON-AFFIRMING-GAY-LESBIAN-BISEXUAL-PERSONS-AND-THEIR-MINISTRIES.pdf.

PART THREE

CREATING A BISEXUALLY HEALTHY CONGREGATION

A bisexually healthy faith community has religious professionals who are educated about bisexuality and can provide pastoral care and preaching that are inclusive of bisexuality. A bisexually healthy congregation addresses bisexuality in sexuality education for youth and adults, in LGBT welcome, and in social action.

WELCOMING AND AFFIRMING BISEXUAL PEOPLE IN CONGREGATIONS

The Religious Institute's vision is for all faith communities to be sexually healthy, just, and prophetic. In its publication *A Time to Build: Creating Sexually Healthy Faith Communities*, the Religious Institute defined a sexually healthy faith community as one "that promotes the integration of sexuality and spirituality in worship, preaching, pastoral care, youth and adult education, and social action programs."[1] The eight building blocks of a sexually healthy congregation are sexually healthy religious professionals, worship and preaching on sexuality issues, sexuality education for youth, sexuality education for adults, welcome and full inclusion for LGBT individuals and families, a commitment to preventing sexual abuse, and social action efforts for sexual justice.

While many progressive denominations and movements have been working to welcome and affirm lesbians and gay men in their congregations, far fewer have worked to explicitly welcome and affirm bisexual people. Too often, the "B" in LGBT is not addressed in faith communities. A bisexually healthy congregation is one where people who identify as bisexual or have bisexual behaviors or attractions hear and see their experiences, concerns, and gifts reflected. This does not mean that a congregation must focus on bisexuality, but that efforts to counter biphobia and bisexual invisibility are apparent in congregational life.

How can faith communities be sure they are welcoming and affirming spaces for bisexual people? Perhaps there are actions you can take right away, as well as other longer-term changes that your community can begin to make, to develop a climate that fully welcomes and includes bisexual people.

In the congregation, religious educators or other leaders can host adult and youth education forums around sexual orientation and gender identity, being sure to engage presenters who are bisexual or bi-friendly and who can address the full range of sexual identity with up-to-date information. Congregations can offer prayer groups or support groups specifically for bisexual individuals, perhaps in collaboration with other faith communities. Congregations can also assess their LGBT programming and groups to determine if bisexual persons are specifically included. The "B" is nearly always included in the LGBT acronym for congregational groups, but the specific gifts and concerns of bisexual persons are often not addressed.

Finally, I confronted the reality that somehow, both of these attractions *did* exist within me. I *was* truly attracted to men…and to women. I sat alone in the stairwell outside my bedroom, my head held in my hands, when the thought entered my consciousness for the first time: maybe I was bisexual. As soon as I'd named it, a homophobic solution came on its heels: I would just decide not to pursue my attraction to women. Ironically, this is pretty much exactly what the Catholic Church tells me to do….I thought I'd arrived at a prudent solution: I could inwardly acknowledge who I really was while also pursuing only love that I could declare publicly, only love that didn't entail the risk of being cast out of my community. But the solution must not have been too great after all, because I fell into the worst depression of my life.

— *Lacey Louwagie, co-editor of* Hungering and Thirsting
for Justice: True Stories by Young Adult Catholics

While many, if not all, of the suggestions below can apply to any group that is marginalized, it is important to name and include bisexual people specifically, as a distinct group in the LGBT community. Consider the following suggestions to assess if they might apply to your congregation.

EDUCATION
- Learn the basics about bisexuality and issues facing bisexual people, and provide opportunities for the congregation to learn and discuss together. (See *Part Four: Resources.*) Consider sharing copies of this guidebook with clergy and lay leaders
- Include bisexuality-related programming on the congregational calendar.
- Host a workshop, panel, adult education forum or other event where bisexual people can share their stories and engage congregants in dialogue. Provide an opportunity for congregants to share their feelings.
- Encourage clergy, pastoral care providers, lay leaders, staff, and religious education volunteers to become familiar with specific concerns of bisexual persons.
- Assure that religious education for middle and high school youth includes sexuality education that affirms bisexuality as a sexual orientation, along with other sexual orientations and gender identities.
- Create opportunities to hear about how faith plays a role in the lives of people in your congregation. A welcoming environment for bisexuals will help ensure that their stories are heard.

CONGREGATIONAL LIFE

- Assume that bisexual people are present in the congregation.

- Recognize that many people do not use the word "bisexual" to identify their sexual identity even if they have behaviors or attractions that might be considered bisexual.

- Respect people's privacy and boundaries, as well as their self-identification with regards to their sexual orientation and/or gender identity. Do not "out" individuals as bisexual without their consent.

- Become an officially-recognized LGBT welcoming congregation through your denomination or movement. Be sure bisexuality and the concerns of bisexual people are included in the process (see "Welcoming Organizations Associated with Denominations and Movements," pp. 92–93).

- Be sure that bisexual people are named in your congregation's welcome statement. (Say lesbian, gay, bisexual and transgender rather than just using "LGBT.") Be sure your welcome statement is well publicized on the congregation's homepage, social media, in the newsletter, in membership materials, in the bulletin, and through other media.

- Don't assume a person's sexual orientation because of the gender or sex of their partner.

- Include bisexual people in the leadership of the congregation.

- Consider ways to observe Bisexuality Day (September 23) in your congregation.[2]

- In trainings and orientations for lay leaders, including worship leaders, membership leaders, greeters and ushers, religious education volunteers, etc., talk about how to create a welcoming environment by using inclusive language and challenging assumptions.

- Honor bisexual people and people with bisexual attractions or behaviors in your worship services where appropriate. If you hold a worship service with an "LGBT" theme, be sure that it is inclusive of bisexuality.

- Assure that referral lists include bi-friendly counselors, therapists, and organizations, listed as such.*

ADVOCACY

- Participate in local events for the bisexual community. If such events do not occur in your community, consider hosting one.

- Assure that information on sexual orientation in your congregation's information rack or other resources is bi-friendly and inclusive.

- Hold a public forum, a panel discussion, or another event open to the public on a topic related to bisexuality and promote it throughout your community.

- Reach out to local LGBT organizations. Find out if they are specifically inclusive of bisexual people and maintain a list of bisexual-friendly organizations.*

* Vetting of local organizations and professionals about their attitudes toward bisexuality must generally be done locally. *Part Four: Resources* offers some good places to start.

Questions for Reflection

1. Why is it important for a faith community to be bisexually healthy? What are some ways in which the faith community is already bisexually healthy? What are areas for improvement?

2. How can the congregation more intentionally acknowledge bisexuality? What are the advantages to doing so? What might be the drawbacks?

3. What type of education does the congregation need to begin to be more bi-inclusive and bi-friendly? How can there be greater awareness and involvement?

4. What are the gifts that people who are bisexual might uniquely offer faith communities?

Notes

1 Rev. Debra W. Haffner, *A Time to Build: Creating Sexually Healthy Faith Communities* (Westport, CT: Religious Institute, 2012).

2 For more information about Bisexuality Day, see http://en.wikipedia.org/wiki/Celebrate_Bisexuality_Day.

BISEXUALLY HEALTHY
RELIGIOUS PROFESSIONALS

Sexually healthy religious professionals (clergy, religious educators, and pastoral counselors) are comfortable with their own sexuality, have the skills to provide pastoral care, religious education, and worship on sexuality issues, and are committed to sexual justice in the congregation and in society at large.[1] Bisexually healthy religious professionals have the knowledge and skills to minister to and with bisexual persons. This includes personal attributes, congregational skills, and community and denominational skills. The checklist on pp. 61–62 lists specific skills in each of these categories.

Most religious leaders have not received adequate ministerial training in human sexuality, and even fewer have had the opportunity to learn about ministering with bisexual persons. Studies published by the Religious Institute show that few clergy and religious professionals feel competent in the area of human sexuality. The *Survey of Religious Progressives: A Report on Progressive Clergy Action and Advocacy for Sexual Justice*[2] found that fewer than half of the progressive clergy surveyed felt that seminary adequately prepared them to deal with sexuality issues in the congregation. *Sex and the Seminary, Preparing Ministers for Sexual Health and Justice* found that most religious professionals can graduate from a seminary, divinity or rabbinical school without taking a single sexuality course.[3]

In the years since these studies, many seminaries have begun to improve their program offerings in sexuality. The list of seminaries designated as sexually healthy and responsible by the Religious Institute has grown from ten to thirty. These seminaries and rabbinical schools represent such traditions as the Episcopal Church, the Presbyterian Church (USA), Reform Judaism, the Unitarian Universalist Association, the United Church of Christ, and the United Methodist Church, as well as non-denominational Christian seminaries. An updated list of sexually healthy and responsible seminaries can be found on the website of the Religious Institute (www.religiousinstitute.org).

In most cases, clergy and religious leaders who wish to improve their competency in ministering with bisexual persons will need to take the initiative to do so. If you are a religious leader, you have taken the first step by reading this guidebook. If you are a person of faith who is interested in helping your congregation to become more bisexually healthy and aware, consider sharing a copy of this guidebook with the leaders (lay and ordained) of your congregation.

The following are strategies for religious professionals to increase their ability to minister effectively with bisexual persons:

SEEK OPPORTUNITIES TO INCREASE KNOWLEDGE ABOUT SEXUALITY AND SEXUAL ORIENTATION

Many religious professionals are not aware of ways to learn more about human sexuality. The Religious Institute offers online courses specifically designed to fill the need for education in human sexuality and spirituality for religious leaders. These courses provide a basic overview of human sexuality including sexual identity, sexual orientation, and gender identity. They also help build religious leaders' congregational skills in pastoral counseling, preaching, and teaching. More information can be found at the Religious Institute website at http://www.religiousinstitute.org/course/.

There are a number of other opportunities for in-person and online learning available for religious professionals who are motivated to improve their overall competence in sexuality. For example, each year, the Center for Family Life Education hosts the National Sex Ed Conference, where sexuality education professionals present on a wide variety of topics. The National Gay and Lesbian Task Force hosts a conference each year called Creating Change. In recent years, the Task Force has increased its offerings that address bisexuality, and the conference includes a spirituality track.

Religious leaders and educators can also receive training in sexuality education from the United Church of Christ and the Unitarian Universalist Association. These denominations have jointly developed *Our Whole Lives* (OWL), a comprehensive lifespan sexuality education curriculum that can be adapted for diverse religious traditions. Training is required to be an OWL facilitator, and provides a good foundation of knowledge and skills on sexuality in a faith- and values-based context. The UUA website has a list of OWL facilitator trainings (currently found at http://www.uua.org/re/owl/18217.shtml).

CREATE OPPORTUNITIES TO HEAR THE STORIES OF BISEXUAL PEOPLE IN THE CONGREGATION

In addition to formal learning opportunities, religious leaders and congregations can seek opportunities to be in conversation with people who publicly identify as bisexual. Religious professionals can signal their openness to such conversations by assuring that bisexuality is specifically mentioned in sermons, congregational communications, and religious education whenever sexual orientation is addressed, and by promoting bisexual awareness with specific resources in the congregation's library and literature rack.

Intentional conversations with bisexual people about the ways in which they experience the sacred as well as oppression and marginalization are an important part of becoming a bisexually healthy faith community. These conversations might be part of small groups in the congregation. However, care should be taken to note the value of people's contributions to such groups as individual people of faith, and not merely representatives of a particular group. An environment that welcomes a person's whole identity into the faith community is essential. A good way to begin to hear the witness of bisexual people of faith is by reading their stories throughout this guidebook and in the books listed in *Part Four: Resources*.

ENGAGE IN THEOLOGICAL REFLECTION ABOUT BISEXUALITY

Religious leaders engage in theological reflection in order to increase their own understanding, to prepare to preach and teach, and to equip themselves to provide effective pastoral counseling. Part Two of this guidebook may provide a starting point for religious professionals to think theologically about the gifts and challenges of bisexual identity. Developing adult religious education programming around sacred texts and tradition as they relate to bisexuality allows congregants to undertake their own theological reflection. It also promotes awareness of one's own biases and shortcomings. Theological reflection equips religious professionals to celebrate the gifts of bisexuality and confidently challenge biphobia from a faith perspective. Consider engaging other clergy and congregations in the community in discussions of theological support for bisexual inclusion and welcome.

RECOGNIZE THE IMPACT OF RACISM, SEXISM, AND HETEROSEXISM ON BISEXUAL PERSONS

Racial, ethnic, and sexual politics, privileges, and oppressions affect individuals' experience of bisexuality. In his book *Rainbow Theology*, the Rev. Dr. Patrick S. Cheng, Associate Professor of Historical and Systematic Theology at Episcopal Divinity School, explains:

> Queer people of color are constantly being asked to choose among multiple identities of race, sexuality, and religion....When they are within an LGBTIQ context...they are often asked to suppress the racial and ethnic aspects of their lives. When they are within communities of color...they are often asked to suppress the sexual and gender identity aspects of their lives. And when they are in communities of faith, they are often asked to suppress the racial, ethnic, sexual, and gender identity aspects of their lives. Thus, for many queer people of color, their multiplicity of identities can lead to a profound sense of fragmentation.[4]

For bisexual persons, this sense of fragmentation can be even more profound, as they are almost always assumed to be lesbian/gay or straight. When bisexual individuals do make their sexual orientation known, they are likely to experience prejudice based on negative stereotypes. They may find that even so-called LGBT groups are not welcoming.

Cultural competence for bisexually healthy religious professionals includes an understanding of the intersections of race, sex, ethnicity, sexual health, and religion. Religious professionals can seek to educate themselves about the ways that oppressions interact in the lives of bisexual people of faith.

CHALLENGE BIPHOBIA IN THE CONGREGATION, DENOMINATION, AND COMMUNITY

There are many ways, both direct and indirect, that religious leaders can challenge negative attitudes and stereotypes about bisexuality and help make their communities more sexually healthy and just. Religious leaders can begin by ensuring that congregational anti-harassment or anti-bullying policies include examples of anti-bisexual comments and behavior. Recognizing that biphobia exists within the LGBT community, religious professionals can discuss bisexuality with gay and lesbian congregants and LGBT groups in the congregation.

Religious leaders can work with other clergy in the community to offer faith-based programming that gives accurate information about bisexuality and explores the gifts and challenges of identifying as bisexual. Congregants and their leaders can speak out and take action on sexual justice issues from a faith perspective that honors bisexual people, and they can encourage their denominations and movements to be more attentive to these issues.

BISEXUALLY HEALTHY RELIGIOUS PROFESSIONALS

The list below provides ideas for religious professionals to assess their knowledge about bisexuality and their competence for ministering to and with bisexual persons.

Personal Attributes

Bisexually healthy religious professionals:
- affirm their own sexual orientation and gender identity and respect the sexual orientation and gender identity of others.
- are knowledgeable about sexual orientation and gender identity including knowledge about bisexuality as a distinct sexual orientation.
- have engaged in theological reflection on bisexuality.
- serve as role models who celebrate the diversity of sexual orientations and gender identities.

Congregational Skills

Bisexually healthy religious professionals:

- are able to provide pastoral counseling to adults and youth who identify as bisexual or who report they have bisexual attractions, fantasies, or behaviors.

- recognize personal prejudices and areas for growth in understanding and acceptance of bisexuality as a distinct sexual orientation.

- are familiar with interpretations of sacred texts and traditions that are helpful for bisexual persons.

- are aware of the impact of racism, sexism, biphobia, and heterosexism on bisexual persons.

- are skillful in addressing gender identities and sexual orientations, including bisexuality, in preaching and teaching.

Community and Denominational Skills

Bisexually healthy religious professionals:

- are knowledgeable about their tradition's teaching and policies on bisexuality.

- challenge and work to change biphobia in their faith community and denomination.

- speak out against biphobia in the public arena and seek opportunities to work with others to promote a positive understanding of bisexuality.

CONSIDERATIONS FOR BISEXUAL RELIGIOUS PROFESSIONALS

A major decision for non-heterosexual religious professionals is whether or not to "come out" to their faith community and their denomination or movement. The decision about whether or not to come out carries unique challenges for bisexual persons, as they may face discrimination from both straight and LGBT communities.

Clergy and religious professionals who identify as bisexual face dilemmas on numerous fronts. Should they be open with an ordination committee, search committee, governing body, or congregation? What is the denomination or movement's stated policy about bisexuality? Is the congregation ready to affirm a bisexual religious professional? Is the person prepared to help educate congregants, colleagues, and officials in the denomination or movement about bisexuality? How does sexuality enrich ministry with others? Is there a support network in place?

The lists in this section give both clergy and congregants points for discussion and thought. Most of these considerations were identified by the bisexual religious leaders who participated in the Religious Institute's colloquium on bisexuality in April of 2013.

I've known that I was attracted to people of both genders for a long, long time. Since long before I knew the word "bisexual" — I remember how excited I was as a teenager to discover that there was actually a word for people like me. As an adult, some of my crushes, dates, relationships, etc. have been with women, and some have been with men. As it happens, the person I fell in love with and have committed to spending the rest of my life with is a (wonderful, amazing) man.

Being out can be tricky for bisexuals because our sexuality is often invisible; bis who are with same-sex partners are often assumed to be gay and bis who are with opposite-sex partners are often assumed to be straight. Plus, bisexuals are sometimes viewed with suspicion or confusion by both ends of the Kinsey scale, gay and straight alike. All of this, coupled with the fact that I hate few things more than awkwardness and making other people feel uncomfortable, has meant that until now, I've been out only in patches: (to) the search committee who hired me, a lot of my friends but not all, and some family members, but not most.

— *Rev. Summer Shaud, Associate Pastor at First Congregational Church in Natick, MA*

Considerations for Coming Out

- Assess your congregation's readiness.

  Make sure the congregation is ready to handle the news well. Are congregants able to discuss sexuality issues openly? Do they understand that sexuality and spirituality are linked in a positive way? Are sexuality issues addressed in sermons and religious education?

- Consider your context (especially if you are in a search process).

  Does your denomination/movement have a specific statement or position about bisexuality? (Most do not; see pp. 47–51.)

- Consider your local governing body.

  Is it more or less bi-inclusive than your larger movement/denomination? Will you have support at the local level if you encounter resistance or intolerance in your denomination or movement?

- Consider your own needs.

  Individuals are unique in terms of what they need in order to experience balance between their internal truth and the way they are perceived/known in the world. How important to your sense of authenticity and well-being is it to be "out"? How many people would you ideally want to have this information about you?

  What would the impact be on your personal well-being and spirituality if you were not "out"? What would the impact be if you *were* "out"?

- Consider the impact on your partner/family.

  Have you and your loved ones discussed how to handle possible negative reactions, comments, and questions from the congregation?

  How would you being "out" impact the way your partner (if you have one) is seen in the world? Do you and/or your partner think it would be positive? Negative?

- Consider social media.

  Are you already out on social media? How will being out on social media sites affect you and your relationship with the congregation?

  Understand that coming out as bisexual may mean having less privacy. As the stories throughout this guide illustrate, coming out as a bisexual religious professional often means facing questions from congregants and colleagues. In many cases, you will be the first person to educate congregants and colleagues about bisexuality.

- Consider the impact on your ministry.

  How will you deal with people who will see you as "the bisexual minister?" Are you prepared to integrate your sexuality into your ministry? Do you have a spiritual director that you trust to be your companion on this journey?

- Be prepared by knowing your boundaries.

  Inevitably, congregants or colleagues will ask questions or make remarks that cross the boundary between ministry and personal life. Have you rehearsed such situations? Are you prepared with kind but firm responses? For example, "As your minister, it's never appropriate for me to discuss my own sexual behaviors. I'm happy to continue the conversation about how sexuality and spirituality are connected for everyone."

Given all the cautions, why would bisexual religious professionals choose to be open about their sexuality in their faith communities? The clergy and religious leaders at the Religious Institute's colloquium on bisexuality related the blessings of the ability to be open with their faith communities.

One young woman recounted her interview with a denominational official as she prepared to go to seminary. She had already been accepted as a candidate for ministry. The official had read her autobiography prior to their conversation. When the interview occurred, the official reported that he was concerned that the young woman's autobiography recounted romantic relationships with women and men. He told her that she would need to "choose." This young woman assumes that at some point on her journey to becoming a minister, she'll have to "declare herself" as either lesbian or straight.

— *Anonymous, personal communication, used with permission*

Bisexual clergy and religious leaders who are able to share openly that they are bisexual can contribute to the sexual health of their congregations and communities. An openly bisexual religious leader can:

- encourage discussion of bisexuality in the congregation and with colleagues.
- create an opportunity to dispel myths and stereotypes while countering biphobia and bisexual invisibility.
- serve as a role model for their congregations about healthy integration of sexuality and spirituality.
- allow congregants who think they may be bisexual to feel less alone.
- encourage all congregants to reflect on their own relationships and orientations.
- let congregants know they can approach them with sexuality concerns.
- can address issues of professional boundaries in the context of health disclosure rather than secrecy.
- model authenticity.

I routinely encounter souls harmed by religion who see my mere existence as an out bisexual rabbi as a beacon of hope. Perhaps most powerful is the opportunity to journey with people who are LGBT or Q at pivotal moments in their lives. It is an honor and it is humbling to experience how liberated people feel when they can explore matters of core significance with someone they trust will see and rejoice in their holiness.

— *Rabbi Debra Kolodny, Executive Director, Nehirim*

Notes

1 Haffner, *Time to Build*.

2 Rev. Debra W. Haffner and Timothy Palmer, "Survey of Religious Progressives," Religious Institute, http://www.religiousinstitute.org/sites/default/files/research_reports/surveyofreligiousprogressivespublicreportapril2009withcover.pdf.

3 Dr. Kate M. Ott, *Sex and the Seminary: Preparing Ministers for Sexual Health and Justice* (Westport, CT: Religious Institute), 2009.

4 Patrick S. Cheng, *Rainbow Theology: Bridging Race, Sexuality, and Spirit* (New York: Seabury Books, 2013), 100.

WORSHIP AND PREACHING

*I*ntentionally celebrating the diversity of sexual identities in worship can help congregants understand that sexual diversity is a sacred gift; that it can be talked about in a respectful and reverent manner; and that that clergy and worship leaders are comfortable addressing sexual diversity in general and bisexuality in particular.

Acknowledging bisexual identities in worship and preaching helps to reduce the invisibility of bisexuality. From the pulpit, faith leaders can make use of "teachable moments" in the media or popular culture to challenge myths and stereotypes about bisexuality. Clergy can demonstrate their "bi-friendliness" by being inclusive of bisexual attractions, feelings and behaviors in their language in worship and preaching. Bisexually healthy worship models the natural integration of sexuality and spirituality in the life of the community.

This section includes a responsive reading, prayer, and hymns that are particularly appropriate for celebrating sexual diversity. All resources in this section may be reproduced for use in worship, with the addition of the following copyright message "© Religious Institute, used by permission."

A READING ON SEXUAL AND GENDER DIVERSITY

We affirm sexual and gender diversity as gifts people offer to their congregations and communities. We urgently call for faith-based approaches that embrace this diversity and advocate justice. Living in a time of rapid social change challenges us all to create loving, respectful relationships and to honor the many ways that people live and love. While most of us may be accustomed to categorizing people as male or female, heterosexual or homosexual, binary thinking fails to reflect the full diversity of human experience and the richness of creation. The courageous witness of lesbian, gay, bisexual and transgender people (LGBT), along with a growing body of social and scientific research, inspire us to affirm sexual and gender diversity as a blessed part of life.

— *Religious Institute, Open Letter to Religious*
Leaders on Sexual and Gender Diversity

RESPONSIVE READING

One: We give thanks for the beauty and wonder of creation.

Many: **We honor the diversity of sexual orientations and gender identities in our world.**

One: We affirm the dignity and worth of all people including those who are bisexual, transgender, gay, or lesbian.

Many: **All persons deserve human rights, equality, and affirmation in their communities.**

One: Moving beyond binaries invites us into the mystery and complexity of human sexuality, and of the Divine.

Many: **Bisexuality reminds us of the diversity, beauty, and wonder of creation.**

One: We respect the dignity and sacred worth of all persons.

Many: **We dedicate ourselves to advocating for bisexual visibility in our congregations and our communities.**

One: We lament the harm done to bisexual people by religious communities and by LGBT communities.

Many: **We commit to loving our neighbors as ourselves and to working for equality and justice for people of all sexual orientations and gender identities.**

One: We affirm the many ways in which human beings form intimate relationships.

Many: **May we work to create a world where all just and loving relationships are celebrated.**

All: **Justice and love flourish when all people can live with integrity and authenticity.**

PRAYER

Holy one, we know you by many names or no name at all, because your mystery and complexity are boundless. Likewise, we have many names for our sexual and gender identities. We give thanks for the diversity of human sexuality. We acknowledge that at times we fall short of honoring that diversity by holding too tightly to divisions and categories. Help us to honor the identities and experiences of all people and to create a world where everyone can live with authenticity and dignity.

A BI-INCLUSIVE READING OF A JEWISH PRAYER

(The L'cha Dodi is a Jewish prayer recited on Friday nights to welcome Shabbat prior to evening services. L'cha Dodi means "come my beloved.")

A Friday night prayer, *L'cha Dodi* begins with someone inviting a beloved to greet the Shabbat Bride: the Shechina/the indwelling presence of G-d, a feminine manifestation of Divinity. The Shechina is returning after a week where tradition imagines her in exile. She is returning to reunite with HaKadosh Baruch Hu, the Holy One of Blessing, a masculine manifestation of Divinity. The repeating refrain is: *L'cha dodi, likrat kallah, pnai Shabbat n'kabbelah.* "Come my beloved, to greet the Bride, we'll welcome the presence of Shabbat."

In this phrase we have a speaker of an unknown gender (woman, man, genderqueer) calling a male beloved (either G-d or a lover or friend) to greet a female G-d manifestation. The relationship between speaker and the one called could be between two men, or a woman and a man, or a genderqueer person and a man.

Liturgy like this that lifts up the multiply gendered identity of G-d is precious in and of itself, but here we see something even more lovely. *L'cha Dodi* invites the possibility of same gender or non-binary gendered love in humans who are in relationship with a multiply/fluidly/complicatedly gendered G-d. For we who hold strongly to the belief that diversity in sexual orientation and gender identity is holy, for we who know that words repeated in community, in prayer, in song go deep into our psycho/spiritual core, helping to define what we believe, this prayer is kind of a miracle. *

— *Rabbi Debra Kolodny, Executive Director, Nehirim*

* Rabbi Kolodny acknowledges that her teacher, Norman Shore, first alerted her to this grammatical possibility.

HYMN: WHEN BODIES JOIN AND SOULS COMBINE

A hymn by Patrick Evans created for the 10th Anniversary
of the Religious Institute. Based on the Religious Declaration
on Sexual Morality, Justice, and Healing

1. When bod-ies join and souls com-bine: this fra-gile dance, a sa - cred art; Cre - a - tor's
2. But bod-ies bound and souls en chained by bi - as, creed or cir - cum stance A - wait the
3. Let bod-ies thrive with souls com bined: no sep - ar - a-tion, no di - vide Of ma - ny
4. We cel - e-brate this bless-ed trust with ho - li - ness, in - te - gri - ty; To name and

gift is Spir-it's sign of love and mys-ter - y and heart. De-lights e -
day to be re-claimed and freed for car-ing con - so - nance. Good peo-ple
gen - dered, ma - ny - signed and ma - ny - hued cre - a - tion wide. I - mage Di -
teach ways that are just, and claim this sa - cred my - ster - y. For lov - ing

merge, for - give-ness flows, en - act - ed or - der of the earth. In sweet em -
all who live and love, and wear the priv' lege of es - teem, Work for a
vine, we, named as good, di - ver - si - ties of life and love, Are held and
un - ion, bless - ed care, for mu - tu - a - li - ty and grace, We of - fer

brace each oth - er knows a ho - ly pleas - ure, bless - ed worth.
world that will re - move the shame-locked doors, the time re - deem.
healed and un - der - stood, and in the Spir - it live and move.
this un - ceas - ing prayer for ev - ery - one in ev - ery place.

8.8.8.8. Tune: THORSON

HYMN: PRAISE THE
SOURCE OF ALL CREATION

(Genesis 1:1-27, 31; Proverbs 3:13–18)

*Hymn text by Jann Aldredge-Clanton, winner of the
Religious Institute's 2012 hymn contest and based on the
Religious Declaration on Sexual Morality, Justice, and Healing.*

Praise the Source of all creation, giving life throughout the Earth,
blessing every love relation, filling all with sacred worth.
Celebrate all forms and colors, varied beauty everywhere,
streams of goodness overflowing, wondrous gifts for all to share.

Many genders, many races, all reflect Divinity;
many gifts and many graces help us be all we can be.
Partners on this path of freedom, taking down each stifling wall,
we will open doors of welcome, bringing hope and joy to all.

Long have many been excluded, judged and scorned by custom's norms;
everyone will be included as we work to bring reforms.
Let us end abuse and violence, bringing justice everywhere,
joining Holy Wisdom's mission, helping all be free and fair.

Equal marriage, healing, freeing, nurtures body, mind and soul,
reaffirming every being, all created good and whole.
Come, rejoice and sing together, celebrating life and love;
praise the great Creative Spirit, living in us and above.

8.7.8.7 D (suggested tunes: HYFRYDOL, BEECHER, HYMN TO JOY)

PASTORAL CARE AND COUNSELING

Clergy, religious leaders, and other pastoral counselors can be prepared to handle the pastoral needs of people who identify as bisexual as well as people who do not identify as bisexual but experience a range of sexual attractions, feelings, or behaviors toward or with people of more than one sex or gender. Some openly bisexual congregants may seek to know that they are accepted and supported by their minister, rabbi or imam. Some congregants may be experiencing sexual attractions and fantasies about people of a different gender identity or biological sex than those to whom they have previously been attracted. They may seek a safe place to explore a changing sense of self or how to deal with those feelings within a committed monogamous sexual relationship. Some people may need pastoral support because their family members have come out to them as bisexual. Parents may notice that their children have attractions to people of more than one sex or gender.

A bisexual 21 year old college student and her minister gave the Religious Institute permission to share their story anonymously.

The congregant from conservative religious background was in her first year of college and had begun questioning her sexuality. A friend referred her to a minister at a church on campus.

"I was very hesitant writing her an email about something that I was so unsure about disclosing. Weeks came around, and I finally had the courage to write that email and several more. The pastor's emails in response assured me of God's love. I had a meeting with her and it was wonderful. She assured me that what I shared would be confidential. She sat there and listened. She waited, allowed me to say what was on my mind, and related to my own hopes, desires, and internal struggles. In our meetings, she always opened up the floor for me to speak, and responded to my requests in an open-minded, prayerful, and friendly fashion."

The pastor in this story stresses that the time spent with this young woman both via email and in person was actually quite minimal (four or five emails and two in-person meetings). However, it made a huge impression on this young woman struggling to deal with the effects of a very conservative theology and its impact on her growing awareness of her bisexuality.

Congregants are most likely to raise issues around bisexuality with a clergyperson or other religious leader if they know the leader is comfortable and open to talking about sexuality and sexual orientation in general, and bisexuality in particular. Clergy can signal their openness by making sure that their language in sermons is inclusive of bisexual persons. Clergy need to avoid assuming or conveying that all congregants are heterosexual or that a congregant with a same-sex partner is automatically gay or lesbian. Openly bisexual speakers can be included in education events, and biphobia (as well as homophobia and transphobia) can be addressed when preaching and teaching on sexual justice. The positive aspects of bisexual experience can also be celebrated in sermons and education events — opening up the possibility of fuller understandings of blessed relationships and of the sacred.

PASTORAL COUNSELING WITH THE PLISSIT MODEL

Many clergy have not been adequately trained to address sexuality issues with congregants, although most have some pastoral counseling training with marriage and family issues. The PLISSIT model was developed almost forty years ago to help health care providers address sexuality needs and concerns in their work.[1] PLISSIT is an acronym that stands for Permission, Limited Information, Specific Suggestions, and Intensive Therapy.[2]

The PLISSIT counseling model can help clergy and religious professionals who are not trained psychologists, psychiatrists, or sex therapists address the pastoral care needs of congregants who have concerns or needs related to bisexuality. These might include:

- congregants who have concerns about their own bisexual attractions or behaviors.
- congregants who have concerns about behaviors of a child, other family member, or friend.
- congregants who identify as bisexual and are seeking affirmation in their religious setting.
- congregants who are partnered with someone who is just discovering a bisexual identity.
- congregants who have discovered a partner's use of erotica that suggests attractions or fantasies to people of a different sex or gender than the congregants' own.

Permission

Permission in the PLISSIT model is short for "permission giving." It gives congregants permission to talk about their sexual feelings, attractions, and behaviors. Permission does not mean telling someone what to do; instead, it means offering congregants a safe space to talk about their concerns about sexuality. Permission giving on bisexuality begins with a welcoming attitude to people of differing sexual orientations. In a pastoral counseling setting, an example of permission giving is letting congregants know that many others experience a non-heterosexual orientation and that attractions, behaviors, and feelings for people of more than one gender or sex are common. Sharing that some people identify as "mostly heterosexual" or "mostly homosexual" while experiencing a wider range of attractions and fantasies may be comforting for some people. It may be useful for clergy to share the information from the "Prevalence of Bisexuality in the United States" and "Myths and Facts About Bisexuality" sections of this guidebook with congregants.

Permission from a clergyperson to accept and name one's sexual orientation can be very powerful for congregants, especially if they have previously understood same-sex feelings to be immoral or sinful. Permission giving can also help congregants understand that their sexuality and their faith are closely connected. This connection can prove very healing to people who have been taught previously that sexuality is not supposed to be a part of their spirituality or their faith.

Permission giving may mean also helping the person understand the difference between attraction, behavior, and identity, and that these aspects of sexuality may differ from one another. For example, a person may be attracted to men and women, but prefer sexual behaviors with men. Or a person may engage in sexual behaviors with men and women, but identify as gay, lesbian, or straight. It can be helpful to some to hear that it is not necessary to label one's sexual orientation or to come out to others as bisexual (or another label of their choosing) until or unless the person is ready or wants to do so. Self-acceptance is often a private thing for people with bisexual attractions, behavior, or identity, and it does not need to be shared with others unless individuals choose to do so. Accepting one's sexual orientation is a process, and religious leaders can let congregants know they are there to listen as congregants sort out what may be new feelings. Religious leaders are there to listen and be supportive, not to direct congregants in any way.

All sexually healthy adults need to understand that there is a difference between having a sexual feeling and acting upon it, and they need to distinguish between sexual behaviors that are life-enhancing and those that might be harmful to self or others.

Pastoral care providers can offer congregants the opportunity to think through their own moral and ethical decisions about how they will express their sexuality. For example, congregants in committed monogamous relationships can be counseled on understanding that being attracted to people of more than one sex does not mean that they have to act on those attractions, and that this self-awareness can be a positive part of their sexuality. Congregants may find it helpful to learn that, contrary to stereotypes, a bisexual orientation does not necessitate having multiple partners or acting on attractions outside one's primary relationship.

Some congregants may need a safe place to explore their feelings that their understanding of their sexual orientation is changing and may continue to change over time. Clergy can help congregants understand that claiming an identity at one time does not necessarily mean that they must hold it forever, while also reinforcing the fact that bisexuality is, for many people, an enduring sexual orientation. Some people may be surprised in mid- to later life to find themselves falling in love with someone of a different sex or gender than their previous partners.

Clergy and other pastoral care providers are not expected to violate their religious beliefs and give permission for behaviors that are counter to them. However, they do have an obligation to listen deeply and to be honest with congregants if their beliefs differ from what is accepted by the majority of sexuality professionals.

Limited Information

Limited information involves providing information to congregants. Clergy and other religious professionals are not expected to be experts in sexual orientation, but should have some basic knowledge to share with bisexual congregants. For example, a pastoral care provider can share information about different models of sexual orientation such as the Klein Sexual Orientation Grid, and explain basic information about gender identity and sexual orientation. (See *Part One: Definitions and Models of Sexual Orientation.*)

Information can be placed in a religious context to facilitate a sense of personal acceptance and ethical decision making. Sharing alternative theological perspectives or Scripture texts that feature people who may have been bisexual might be helpful. (See *Part Two: Sacred Texts and Religious Traditions.*)

In addition, clergy can help congregants decide whether to disclose information about their bisexuality and how much information they want to share with significant others, family members, children, and the faith community. Many bisexual people will want to feel publicly affirmed by their faith community, while others, particularly as they are sorting out their feelings and their decisions about sexual and romantic relationships, may choose to keep this information private. All individuals are unique in terms of what they need in order to experience balance between their internal truth and the way they are perceived/known in the world. Choosing to remain private or to tell a limited number of people about one's bisexual attractions, behavior, or identity does not mean a person is inauthentic. The religious leader can keep the door open for future discussions: "Know that I'm here to talk more about this with you at a future time."

Specific Suggestions

Specific suggestions means offering concrete steps and ways for congregants to continue to develop accepting attitudes about their own sexuality. For bisexual congregants, this may mean referring them to bi-friendly LGBT groups[3] in the community or in the church, introducing them to openly bisexual people in the congregation who have expressed willingness to be a resource for others, and providing books and websites for more information. Clergy should have a referral list of local and national organizations that address bisexuality. (See *Part Four: Resources.*) Clergy should also have a list of referrals for people who discover that their primary partners are having fantasies, attractions, or relationships with people of a different sex or gender than they are – for example, a heterosexual woman who discovers gay erotica on her husband's computer or a gay man who discovers his spouse is having an affair with a woman. Organizations like Transcending Boundaries[4] address options for these types of "mixed marriages."

Depending on the comfort level, skill, and training of the pastoral care provider and the counseling relationship, clergy could help people explore how they will address their bisexual orientation while honoring the commitments they have made to a primary partner. This could include bringing up whether the use of fantasy, sexually explicit materials, and role playing might be acceptable for a monogamous couple where one or both partners are bisexual.

Intensive Therapy

Intensive therapy is beyond the scope of pastoral care and counseling. Some individuals may experience serious distress around their bisexuality. Bisexual people are at especially high risk for feeling isolated, as many myths and stereotypes persist about bisexuality, and bisexual people are often marginalized in both straight and LGBT communities. For some individuals, coping with these issues can cause depression, anxiety disorders, or even suicidal thoughts. Every clergyperson needs to have a reliable referral list of mental health providers and services in the community. Clergy and religious leaders should try to include bi-friendly therapists on this referral list. For congregants who have specific issues related to their sexual orientation beyond the skills of the clergyperson, the American Association of Sexuality Educators, Counselors, and Therapists (AASECT) provides a list of certified sexuality therapists and counselors by state at www.aasect.org.

Questions for Reflection

1. Would congregants be comfortable going to a religious leader in the congregation to discuss their bisexual identity, attractions, or behaviors? If not, how would the religious leader obtain additional training?

2. What does "permission giving" mean in the context of pastoral counseling? Why is "permission giving" important in pastoral counseling around sexuality issues, including congregants who identify as bisexual?

3. What are some resources for clergy and other religious leaders can use to obtain factual information for congregants who identify as bisexual? Where can clergy and religious leaders find information about their faith tradition that will be helpful to those who identify as bisexual?

4. Does the congregation have a referral list of qualified mental health professionals who are bi-friendly? How might such a list be developed?

Notes

1 Jack S. Annon,"The PLISSIT model: a proposed conceptual scheme for the behavioral treatment of sexual problems," *Journal of Sexuality Education and Therapy* 2 no. 2 (1976): 1–15.

2 The PLISSIT model was adapted for religious professionals by Haffner, *Time to Build*.

3 Bisexual people are marginalized and oppressed within the LGBT community as well as outside of it. Be sure to vet the bi-friendliness of any LGBT organization you recommend by speaking to someone from the organization candidly about its affirmation of bisexuality as a valid sexual orientation.

4 Mark Rheault, "Mixed Orientation Marriage: Introduction to Mixed Orientation Marriages," Transcending Boundaries 2014, http://www.transcendingboundaries.org/resources/mixed-orientation-marriage.html.

YOUTH

*F*orming a sexual identity is a key developmental task for all adolescents. During adolescence, young people begin to develop a sense of their own sexual orientation and gender identity. Young teens typically begin to experience their first erotic attractions, and many begin to engage in sexual behaviors by middle adolescence. Youth who embrace a lesbian, gay, bisexual, or transgender identity can face a number of challenges from family, friends, school, and faith communities, and for bisexual adolescents, these challenges can be magnified.

Teens who experience attractions and/or romantic feelings to people of more than one gender or sex can feel marginalized by peers and face discrimination and even violence from adults. If teenagers have erotic dreams, fantasies, or other attractions about people of a different sex or gender than they had assumed they were attracted to, they may feel frightened, alone, and anxious. Religious educators, clergy, and congregations can help young people feel valued, loved, and safe as they form their sexual identities.

Angelus Ferroro (a pseudonym for a 17-year-old from New Jersey), writes about being bisexual for the website sexetc.org. (Used with permission.)

I often find it difficult to date. I never know if I should wait to tell whomever I am dating about my sexuality in the beginning, or if I should wait and see how the relationship progresses. I often wish I could be completely honest at all times, but the reality is people are not as accepting as we would wish them to be. By lying we are hiding our true selves and trying to protect ourselves from being shunned by both sexes.

I find it difficult to constantly be told by some heterosexuals, gays, and lesbians that I need to "pick a team" and stick with it. The scrutiny from others has led me to question myself further. But in being honest with myself, I have learned that I am attracted to both sexes, and if the person I fancy cannot accept that, then he or she is not worth my time.

As we discover our sexual identities, we may encounter issues of discrimination and intolerance head-on. Adolescence is not only an emotional roller coaster, it's also a time when your sexual identity begins to form. Why should it be repressed? Your sexual orientation — straight, gay, or bi — is part of who you are. Accept it. Love it.

According to a 2011 report from the U.S. Centers for Disease Control, the prevalence of health-risk behaviors such as violence, attempted suicide, alcohol use, and other drug use among students who identify as bisexual or who have sexual contact with more than one sex is higher than the prevalence of those same behaviors among heterosexual or gay/lesbian students.[1]

More teenagers than in the past may be engaging in sexual behaviors with people of different sexes. This is especially true for teenage girls. Although only 1 to 1.5% of teen boys in the most recent studies report engaging in sexual behaviors with both sexes, 6 to 8% of teen girls do. Some hypothesize that this reflects a cultural "bisexual chic" among teen girls as reflected in teen-oriented popular media. Others believe that as the culture becomes more open and accepting of bisexuality, more young people are able to affirm that they experience a range of sexual attractions.

Some young people are now identifying as bisexual as early as middle school. According to the American Academy of Pediatrics, "young people are recognizing their sexual orientation earlier than in the past..."[2] In a 2013 study of LGBT adults, the median age that respondents who identified as bisexual say they first thought they were not straight was 13.[3] The median age at which bisexual respondents in this study said they were sure of their sexual orientation was 17.[4]

Congregations should be aware that among today's teenagers, many adolescents who experience sexual and romantic attraction to more than one gender or sex believe that the word "bisexual" does not adequately describe their sexual orientation. As noted in *Part One: Bisexuality Basics*, many people (including youth) who are attracted to people of more than one gender or sex do not use the word *bisexual* to describe themselves. Supporting young people as they begin to discover their sexual identities involves allowing them to name (or choose not to name) those identities. People who have attractions to people of different genders or sexes may use terms like fluid, pansexual, queer, or omnisexual. Some youth groups use the acronym "GLOW," which stands for "gay, lesbian, or whatever." Some adolescents may not feel a need or may not be ready to label themselves or their behaviors. Still others may claim a bisexual, fluid, or queer identity as teens and then identify differently when they become adults.

In every congregation, some young people will be exploring whether they are gay, straight, bisexual, or another orientation during their teen years. Some of these youth may grow up to identify as bisexual, some as gay or lesbian, and some as straight. The box reprinted on the next page with permission from Advocates for Youth is taken from a pamphlet on bisexuality written by youth, and may give you some ideas for how to answer a teen who asks, "How do I know if I'm bisexual?"

How Do I Know If I'm Bisexual?

There is a lot of confusion at first. Society teaches that people can only be one way or the other [gay or straight] or that bisexuality is a stage or a phase, and one doesn't stay there for very long. But once past the confusion, you'll know you are bisexual as surely as your pal knows she's straight and your other pal knows he's gay.

— *Eric, Colorado, age 24*

I always knew I was attracted to women, but I felt a pull towards men as well.

— *Suzanna, Maryland, age 17*

Determining your sexuality can be highly confusing. Teenagers often feel a lot of pressure to choose to define themselves as being heterosexual or homosexual. You might feel that you do not fit either of these categories, and you may notice that you are "turned on" and have sexual feelings about people of your own gender and another gender. These feelings may indicate you will identify as bisexual. Keep in mind, however, that you do not have to prove you are bisexual. There is no *test* for bisexuality.

A bisexual person may have one committed relationship that lasts for decades. Many bisexual people have no sexual relationships or have these relationships with people of only one gender; yet, they still consider themselves bisexual. Some people have relationships with people of their own and of another gender, yet do not identify as bisexual. It all comes down to what makes you feel most comfortable and what you perceive yourself to be. Don't worry about not knowing for sure. Sexuality develops over time, and you should feel no pressure to identify in any particular way.

— *Advocates for Youth, "How Do I Know If I'm Bisexual,"*
http://www.advocatesforyouth.org/publications/publications-a-z/
724-i-think-i-might-be-bisexual-now-what-do-i-do (Used with permission)

Questions that teens may want to explore with their minister, youth group leader, or in a youth group setting include:

- Who should I tell that I'm bisexual?
- When or how should I come out to my parents? My family? My teachers? My faith community? My friends? People I'm dating?
- How can I be physically safer? How can I be sexually safer?
- Where or how can I meet other bisexual teenagers?
- Can I have a happy, successful life as a bisexual person?

Sexually healthy congregations and religious professionals have an obligation to help young people understand, affirm, and embrace their sexuality.[5] Support for adolescents who are exploring a possible bisexual orientation includes the same elements that need to be in place to support all adolescents, while assuring that bisexuality is not invisible.

Congregations can:

- provide comprehensive sexuality education in the context of faith and values that acknowledges the wide range of sexual orientations, including explicit mention of bisexuality as a distinct sexual orientation.
- provide accurate and up to date information on sexual orientation, including bisexuality, in the youth group space and congregational libraries.
- use bi-inclusive language in worship and teaching settings.
- be sure that straight, gay and lesbian, and bisexual people are explicitly included when sexual orientation is discussed with youth.
- require that youth leaders are trained about sexuality issues, including examining their own attitudes and values about bisexuality. Be sure they can address common myths and stereotypes.
- discuss how gay, lesbian, and bisexual teens can come out safely in your congregation (if they decide to do so).
- help teens explore whether or how to reveal their sexual orientation — whether bisexual, gay, straight, or other — with their families or parents. Offer to help them by role playing or offering to meet with families as they disclose this information.
- have groups for parents of bisexual teens, or explicitly name them in groups for parents of gay, lesbian, bisexual, transgender and questioning teens.
- support proms or alternative social events for LGBT students, welcoming people to bring partners of diverse sexes and genders.
- create a discussion group for teens who are attracted to people of multiple genders or sexes.
- assure that the youth group space is affirming of all queer youth. Does it have a rainbow flag (or a bisexual flag)[6] or safe space[7] stickers? Are there pamphlets from local LGBT organizations, including resources for bisexual teens? For more information on creating a welcoming physical environment for LGBT youth, see the Religious Institute's Acting Out Loud online guide at http://www.religiousinstitute.org/acting-out-loud/.
- specifically name bisexual people (rather than using the LGBT acronym) in anti-discrimination, anti-harassment, and anti-bullying policies.

Questions for Reflection

1. Does the faith community provide sexuality education for adolescents? Does this education address sexual orientation, including bisexuality? Is it taught by trained leaders?

2. Would youth exploring their sexual identity and wondering about bisexuality feel comfortable talking to one of the clergy or youth leaders in the faith community? Why or why not? If not, how can the faith community improve?

3. Would a youth who identifies as bisexual or who has bisexual attractions or behaviors feel affirmed in the youth group? How can the environment offer welcome and support?

Notes

1 Centers for Disease Control and Prevention, *Sexual Identity*.

2 Barbara L. Frankowski, MD, MPH, and Committee on Adolescence, "Sexual Orientation and Adolescents," Pediatrics 113:6 (2004): 1827–1832.

3 Pew Research Center, *Survey of LGBT Americans*, http://www.pewsocialtrends.org/2013/06/13/a-survey-of-lgbt-americans/.

4 Ibid.

5 Religious Institute, *"An Open Letter to Religious Leaders on Adolescent Sexuality,"* Religious Institute on Sexual Morality, Justice, and Healing, http://www.religiousinstitute.org/wp-content/uploads/2009/06/OL-Adolescent-Sexuality.pdf.

6 For more information about the bisexual pride flag, see http://en.wikipedia.org/wiki/Bisexual_pride_flag.

7 For more information and to obtain safe space stickers, see http://safespace.glsen.org/.

SOCIAL ACTION

Almost all faith communities have strong traditions of community service and involvement in social justice in the public arena. Sexually healthy faith communities offer prophetic witness on sexual justice in society as a whole. Policy makers and the public need to hear religious voices on sexual justice issues. Bisexually healthy faith communities and religious leaders can play an important role in challenging damaging stereotypes about bisexual persons and addressing the particular concerns of bisexuals in discussions of issues and policies at all levels.

Many people surmise that if a person is bisexual, they can choose to be involved with a partner of the same or another sex. While the argument that being gay or lesbian is not a choice has been useful in advocating for policies and legislation that benefit gay and lesbian people, this tactic can be problematic for activists on issues that affect people whose sexual orientation may be more fluid. The gay/lesbian community and its allies have not always been aware of the impact of their activism on bisexual people.

Advocating for justice, equality, and rights for bisexual persons can help a congregation:

- demonstrate support for bisexual people both in the congregation and in the community.
- increase its visibility in the community as one that embraces the complexity of sexuality and sexual identity.
- work with multifaith partners to present bisexual-inclusive religious positions on issues.
- engage members in community activism and witness for bisexual visibility.
- provide an example of a progressive religious point of view on sexuality.

A congregation can begin its involvement in social action for bisexual persons by researching the denomination's policies on LGBT issues to see if they address bisexuality (see "Denominational Statements on Bisexuality," pp. 47–51). Congregations can also check with the welcoming organization for their denomination or movement to see if they have specific materials and information on welcoming bisexual persons in faith communities. (See the list of welcoming organizations in *Part Four: Resources.*)

Congregations and social justice/outreach committees can also conduct a variety of activities to advocate for bisexual rights and visibility. For example, they can:

- conduct letter writing/email campaigns about legislation that affects bisexual persons.

- hold community forums and participate in school board meetings, and local and state legislative hearings and community rallies.

- assure that information that is displayed or published in congregational media about advocacy for LGBT rights includes the particular concerns of bisexual people.

- encourage clergy to advocate for visibility and rights for bisexual people when appropriate. This could include appearing in electronic media, being interviewed, and writing op-ed pieces for the local paper.

The following are examples of issues that provide "teachable moments" about bisexuality in communities. Advocacy for bisexual justice and visibility could be accomplished through sermons and education in the faith community, and clergy and religious leaders can speak out in the media or submit op-eds on these issues to their local papers. Other communications and media tools like blogs and social media are avenues to advocate for bisexual justice and visibility as well. Think creatively about how the faith community can be a prophetic voice.

POLICIES THAT AFFECT BISEXUAL PEOPLE

There are public policy issues that affect bisexual people. While most progressive faith communities and religious leaders are aware of how to advocate in the public arena for policies and legislation that benefit gay and lesbian persons, many have not had the opportunity to consider how such activism includes or fails to include bisexuals. Advocating for the rights and recognition of bisexual persons in policies about adoption, immigration, marriage, and youth services helps to promote health and well-being. Consider these ideas for being a more bisexually healthy activist on issues of public policy.

- **Employment non-discrimination:** Advocate for language that specifically names bisexual people and/or that broadens the scope of non-discrimination to all gender identities and sexual orientations. Encourage job protection for bisexual persons through policies that do not presume a person's sexual orientation based on the sex of their spouse/partner.

- **Marriage equality:** Encourage framing the question as one of human rights; encourage the use of the terms "marriage equality" rather than "gay marriage," "same-sex couples" rather than "gay and lesbian couples," and a definition of marriage that is not based on the sex of the people in the relationship.

- **Healthcare:** Advocate for the availability of reproductive healthcare for individuals of all sexual orientations as well as same-sex and other-sex couples. Advocate for culturally competent and sensitive health care for people of all sexual orientations in which providers avoid assumptions about behavior or risk based on a person's identity or sexual partners.

- **Youth:** Youth who are attracted to people of more than one gender or sex are disproportionately affected by bullying, homelessness, and poverty. Advocate for LGBT organizations to include programming and services especially for bisexual youth, for safe spaces that specifically include bisexual youth, and for trainings that include accurate information on bisexuality as a distinct sexual orientation.

- **Immigration and adoption:** Advocate for policies that go beyond immigration and adoption rights for same-sex couples to include other-sex couples where one or both persons openly identify as bisexual.

❧

BEING A GOOD BI ALLY: COMBATTING BIPHOBIA

- Speak up when LGBT welcome is discussed to make sure the concerns of bisexual persons are included.
- Challenge bisexual invisibility and negative stereotypes about bisexual people in the media, the faith community, and the denomination.
- Participate in local events for the bisexual community as a representative of the faith community. If such events do not occur in your community, consider hosting one.
- Assure that information on sexual orientation in your congregation's information rack or other resources is bi-friendly and inclusive.
- Use language that is inclusive of bisexual people.
- Respect the way people identify and use their preferred terms. Avoid questioning people about the "validity" of their identity.
- Set aside assumptions about a person's sexual orientation based on the sex or gender of their partner.
- Be aware that there is not one way of being bisexual. Educate yourself about the variety of bisexual experience.
- Be a good bi-stander. Speak up when someone makes jokes or inappropriate comments about people who are bisexual. Respond to myths and stereotypes.

Questions for Reflection

1. Why is it important for faith leaders and communities to include bisexuality in their social justice work?

2. Consider the issues presented as "teachable moments." Has the faith community taken a stand on any of these issues? How might it include advocacy for bisexual rights and justice?

3. What other issues could include bisexual advocacy? How does faith inform positions on these issues?

A CALL TO ACTION

*P*eople of faith have an obligation to create a world that embraces the diversity of God's creation.

We urge religious leaders and congregations to:

- educate themselves and their faith communities on the diversity of human sexuality and gender identities through age-appropriate sexuality education.

- obtain training and support to address the pastoral needs of congregants who identify as bisexual or who have bisexual attractions or behaviors.

- use the pulpit and public podium to acknowledge the complex realities of sexual orientation, to advocate for full inclusion and acceptance of people of all sexual orientations and gender identities, and to condemn discrimination and violence.

- advocate for bisexual rights and recognition in the LGBT movement and in denominations' inclusion and social justice programs.

- encourage congregations to engage in a formal welcoming program and to ensure that such programs address bisexuality.

- work within their denominations and multifaith organizations for sexual justice and the full inclusion of bisexual persons in every aspect of community life, including ordination, family recognition, and rites of passage.

- publicly advocate for the civil rights of bisexual persons through such avenues as anti-discrimination laws, marriage equality, and access to healthcare.

- develop partnerships with community and national organizations that promote justice and health for bisexual persons.

- acknowledge and support religious leaders, individuals, and communities who have embraced and who represent the diversity of sexualities and gender identities.

Part Four

RESOURCES

There are many resources that can help religious leaders and congregations increase their understanding of bisexuality. The resources that follow include books, organizations, websites, and articles on bisexuality. Updated resources on faith and bisexuality are available at www.religiousinstitute.org.

REPORTS

The Religious Institute is grateful to the authors of the following reports on bisexuality. They provided a starting point for strategies for combatting biphobia and effectively welcoming and affirming bisexual persons in society.

Bisexual Invisibility: Impact and Recommendations
City & County of San Francisco Human Rights Commission, http://www.sf-hrc.org/Modules/ShowDocument.aspx?documentid=989

Bisexual People in the Workplace Guide: Practical Advice for Employers
Brent Chamberlain and Professor Gill Valentine, Stonewall Workplace Guides, http://www.stonewall.org.uk/other/startdownload.asp?openType=forced&documentID=2976

The Bisexuality Report: Bisexual Inclusion in LGBT Equality and Diversity
Meg Barker et al, The Open University Centre for Citizenship, Identities and Governance and Faculty of Health and Social Care, http://www8.open.ac.uk/ccig/files/ccig/The%20BisexualityReport%20Feb.2012.pdf

ORGANIZATIONS

American Institute of Bisexuality
The American Institute of Bisexuality encourages, supports and assists research and education about bisexuality, through programs likely to make a material difference and enhance public knowledge, awareness and understanding about bisexuality. http://www.americaninstituteofbisexuality.org/

Bisexual Resource Center
The BRC is the oldest national bi organization in the U.S. that advocates for bisexual visibility and raises awareness about bisexuality throughout the LGBT and straight communities. http://biresource.net

BiNet USA
BiNet USA facilitates the development of a cohesive network of independent bisexual and bi-friendly communities; promotes bisexual, pansexual and bi-inclusive visibility; and collects and distributes educational information regarding sexual orientation and gender identity with an emphasis on the bisexual and pansexual and allied communities. http://www.binetusa.org

Transcending Boundaries
Transcending Boundaries, Inc. was founded in 2001 to provide education, activism, and support for persons whose sexuality, gender, sex, or relationship style do not fit within conventional categories. The organization serves our ever-evolving communities, including bisexual, pansexual, asexual, fluid, queer, transgender, transsexual, genderqueer, intersex, polyamorous, and kinky persons, as well as allies and those who prefer not to use labels. http://www.transcendingboundaries.org/home/about.html

ONLINE RESOURCES

These links are current as of 2014. To keep up to date, visit www.religiousinstitute.org

Advocates for Youth
"I Think I Might be Bisexual, Now What Do I Do?"
http://www.advocatesforyouth.org/publications/publications-a-z/
724-i-think-i-might-be-bisexual-now-what-do-i-do.

BiMagazine.org
http://bimagazine.org/
A project of the American Institute of Bisexuality: bisexuality in the news,
arts & literature, music, film & TV, and theater.

Bisexual.org
http://www.bisexual.org
An informational and testimonial website of the American Institute of Bisexuality.

Interweave Continental (related organization of the UUA)
"The Bisexuality Curriculum,"
http://interweavecontinental.ning.com/curricula.

Margaret Robinson, "Bisexual Women and Lesbians: Five Survival Tips"
http://www.margaretrobinson.com/journalism/other/survival_tips.html.

More Light Presbyterians, "More Light on Bisexuality"
http://www.mlp.org/wp-content/uploads/2012/04/MLonBi.pdf.

National Gay and Lesbian Task Force, Institute for Welcoming Resources
Many links on faith (mostly Christian) and bisexuality,
http://www.welcomingresources.org/bisexuality.xml.

Rainbow Health Ontario, "Bisexual Health Fact Sheet"
http://www.rainbowhealthontario.ca/admin/contentEngine/
contentDocuments/Bisexual_Health.pdf.

Unitarian Universalist Association, "Bisexuality 101"
http://www.uua.org/lgbtq/identity/25346.shtml

United Church of Christ, "bi-sex' u-al: A Position of Faith"
Curriculum and DVD
http://www.ucc.org/lgbt/resources.html

ARTICLES

Edwards, Rev. Dr. Janet, "Top Five Questions Asked About Being
A Bisexual Minister," *The Huffington Post Religion*,
http://www.huffingtonpost.com/rev-dr-janet-edwards/
top-five-questions-asked-about-being-a-bisexual-minister_b_1280433.html.

Kolodny, Debra, "Bisexuality — Theology and Politics." *Tikkun Magazine*,
July/August 2010.
http://www.tikkun.org/nextgen/bisexuality-theology-and-politics.

Louwagie, Lacey, "Bisexual and Whole," Dignity USA, 3rd Quarter 2012 —
Quarterly Voice, http://www.dignityusa.org/qv/3rd-quarter-2012-quarterly-voice.

Ochs, Robyn, "Biphobia: It Goes More than Two Ways," B. A. Firestein (Ed.)
Bisexuality: The Identity and Politics of an Invisible Minority, Sage Publications,
1996.

BOOKS

Cheng, Patrick S. *Rainbow Theology: Bridging Race, Sexuality, and Spirit.* New York:
Seabury Books, 2013.

Diamond, Lisa M. *Sexual Fluidity: Understanding Women's Love and Desire.*
Cambridge, MA: Harvard University Press, 2009.

Douglas, Kelly Brown. *Black Bodies and the Black Church: A Blues Slant.* Palgrave
Macmillan, Hampshire, UK: 2012.

Drinkwater, Gregg, Joshua Lesser, David Shneer, editors, and Judith Plaskow. *Torah
Queeries: Weekly Commentaries on the Hebrew Bible.* New York: NYU Press, 2009.

Ellison, Marvin M. *Making Love Just: Sexual Ethics for Perplexing Times.*
Minneapolis: Fortress Press, 2012.

Guest, Deryn, Robert Goss, Mona West, and Thomas Bohache, editors.
The *Queer Bible Commentary.* Norwich, UK: SCM Press, 2006.

Hutchins, Loraine and Lani Kaahumanu, editors. *Bi Any Other Name: Bisexual
People Speak Out.* Alyson Books, 1991.

Hutchins, Loraine and H. Sharif Williams, editors. *Sexuality, Religion and the Sacred:
Bisexual, Pansexual and Polysexual Perspectives.* London: Routledge, 2011.

Jung, Patricia Beattie and Darryl W. Stephens, editors. *Professional Sexual Ethics:
A Holistic Ministry Approach.* Minneapolis: Fortress Press, 2013.

Klein, Fritz, MD. *The Bisexual Option, Second Edition.* London: The Haworth Press,
1993.

Kolodny, Debra R. *Blessed Bi Spirit: Bisexual People of Faith*. New York: Bloomsbury Academic, 2000.

Kundtz, David J. and Bernard S. Schlager. *Ministry Among God's Queer Folk: LGBT Pastoral Care*. Cleveland: The Pilgrim Press, 2007.

Louwagie, Lacey. "Where I First Met God." *Unruly Catholic Women Writers: Creative Responses to Catholicism*. Jeana DelRosso, Leigh Eicke and Ana Kothe, editors. New York: SUNY Press, 2013.

Ochs, Robyn. *Getting Bi: Voices of Bisexuals Around the World, Second Edition*. Bisexual Resource Center, 2009.

Palmer, Timothy, and Rev. Debra W. Haffner. *A Time To Seek: A Study Guide on Sexual and Gender Diversity*. Westport, CT: Religious Institute on Sexual Morality, Justice, and Healing, 2007.

Rust, Paula C. Rodriguez, editor. *Bisexuality in the United States*. New York: Columbia University Press, 2000.

FAITH-BASED LGBT RIGHTS ORGANIZATIONS

Believe Out Loud
http://www.believeoutloud.com/

GLAAD's Religion, Faith & Values Program
http://www.glaad.org/programs/faith

Human Rights Campaign, Issue: Religion and Faith
http://www.hrc.org/issues/religion.asp

Many Voices: A Black Church Movement for Gay & Transgender Justice
http://www.manyvoices.org/

National Gay and Lesbian Task Force, Institute for Welcoming Resources
http://www.welcomingresources.org

Other Sheep: Multicultural Ministries with Sexual Minorities in Latin America
Otras Ovejas: Ministerios Multiculturales con Minorias Sexuales
http://www.othersheep.org/

Religious Institute
http://www.religiousinstitute.org

Soulforce
http://soulforce.com/

WELCOMING ORGANIZATIONS ASSOCIATED WITH DENOMINATIONS AND MOVEMENTS

American Baptist Churches USA
Association of Welcoming & Affirming Baptists
http://www.wabaptists.org/

Church of the Brethren / Mennonites
Brethren Mennonite Council for Lesbian, Gay, Bisexual and Transgender Interests
http://www.bmclgbt.org/

Christian Church (Disciples of Christ)
Gay, Lesbian and Affirming Disciples Alliance, Inc. (GLAD)
http://gladalliance.org/site/open-affirming-ministries/

Community of Christ
The Welcoming Community Network
http://welcomingcommunitynetwork.org/

Episcopal Church
Integrity USA
http://www.integrityusa.org/

Evangelical Christians (nondenominational)
The Evangelical Network http://www.t-e-n.org/
Evangelicals Concerned Inc. http://ecinc.org/

Evangelical Lutheran Church in America
ReconcilingWorks: Lutherans for Full Participation
http://www.reconcilingworks.org

Judaism
Keshet: http://www.keshetonline.org/
Nehirim: http://www.nehirim.org/

Church of Jesus Christ of Latter-Day Saints
Affirmation LGBT Mormons Families & Friends
http://www.affirmation.org/

Presbyterian Church USA
Covenant Network of Presbyterians: http://www.covnetpres.org/
More Light Presbyterians: http://www.mlp.org/

Reformed Church in America
Room for All
http://roomforall.com/

Roman Catholic Church
Dignity USA: Gay, Lesbian, Bisexual & Transgender Catholics
http://dignityusa.org

Seventh-Day Adventist
Kinship International
http://www.sdakinship.org/

United Church of Christ
UCC Coalition for LGBT Concerns
http://www.ucccoalition.org/

United Methodist Church
Affirmation: United Methodists for Lesbian, Gay, Bisexual,
Transgender and Queer People: http://www.umaffirm.org/
Reconciling Ministries Network: http://www.rmnetwork.org

Unitarian Universalist Association
For denominational resources: http://www.uua.org/lgbtq
Standing on the Side of Love: Harnessing Love's Power
to Stop Oppression: http://standingonthesideoflove.org
Interweave Continental: http://interweavecontinental.ning.com/

These resources are up to date as of June 2014. Please let us know of additional organizations, books, and online resources on bisexuality. Send your suggestions to info@religiousinstitute.org. Thank you.

ABOUT THE RELIGIOUS INSTITUTE

*F*ounded in 2001, the Religious Institute is a national, multifaith organization dedicated to promoting sexual health, education and justice in faith communities and society. The Religious Institute partners with clergy and congregations, denominations, seminaries, national advocacy organizations, and sexual and reproductive health communities to promote:

- sexually healthy faith communities.
- full equality of women and of lesbian, gay, bisexual and transgender persons in congregations and communities.
- marriage equality.
- comprehensive sexuality education.
- reproductive justice.
- a responsible approach to adolescent sexuality.
- sexual abuse prevention.
- HIV/AIDS education and prevention.
- global sexual health.

The mission of the Religious Institute is to develop a new understanding of the relationship between religion and sexuality. This mission involves:

- developing and supporting a network of clergy, religious educators, theologians, ethicists and other religious leaders committed to sexual justice.
- building the capacity of religious institutions and clergy to provide sexuality education within the context of their faith traditions.
- helping congregations, seminaries and denominations to become sexually healthy faith communities.
- educating the public and policymakers about a progressive religious vision of sexual morality, justice, and healing.

The Religious Institute's network includes more than 15,000 religious leaders and people of faith from more than 70 faith traditions who are committed to sexual health, education, and justice in faith communities and society.

ABOUT THE AUTHORS

MARIE ALFORD-HARKEY is the Deputy Director of the Religious Institute. She is a board member of Integrity Connecticut, and a provincial coordinator for Integrity USA. She earned a Master of Divinity degree from Episcopal Divinity School in 2010 and a Master of Arts degree in French literature from Wayne State University. An educator with 20 years of experience, she taught French and Spanish in public secondary schools for the first twenty years of her career.

DEBRA W. HAFFNER is the Co-founder and President of the Religious Institute. An AASECT certified sexuality educator, she graduated from Union Theological Seminary and the Yale School of Public Health and is an ordained Unitarian Universalist minister. She is the co-creator of the Religious Declaration on Sexual Morality, Justice, and Healing. She is the author or co-author of seven books and many monographs for congregations on sexual health. In 2011, Widener University awarded her a Doctorate of Public Service, h.c.

NOTES